Where was the Church when the youth exploded?

BOOKS BY STUART BRISCOE . . .

The Fullness of Christ
Living Dangerously

Where was the Church when the youth exploded?

by D. STUART BRISCOE

Foreword by Cliff Barrows

ZONDERVAN PUBLISHING HOUSE
OF THE ZONDERVAN CORPORATION
GRAND RAPIDS, MICHIGAN 49506

To Jill by, with and from whom many
of the lessons of this book were learned.

WHERE WAS THE CHURCH WHEN THE YOUTH EXPLODED?
Copyright © 1972 by The Zondervan Corporation
Grand Rapids, Michigan

Library of Congress Catalog Card Number 72-83879

Second printing   December, 1972
Third printing   April, 1973

Printed in the United States of America

CONTENTS

FOREWORD

If you are looking for pat answers – conscience soothers – or clever cliches, *don't read this book!*

On the other hand, an accurate understanding of the "hangups" of today's youth generation is necessary for the church in order to offer a solution to these problems, and introduce a "life-style" in Christ that is both dynamic and demanding.

Where Was the Church When the Youth Exploded? combines spiritual observations and conclusions with practical suggestions for the pastor, the parent, and the youth as well.

Stuart's background in a layman's world in both Europe and America, and his experience with young people qualify him in a unique and practical way to discuss these issues. I've seen him at close range—in our home and community—and the principles he sets forth in this book *really work!*

He has the happy faculty of making people thirsty for what he has—a vital personal relationship with the Living Christ. I frankly admit that his writings, his preaching, and his friendship have done this for me. But this shouldn't be so surprising. Isn't this what "salty" Christians should do?

—CLIFF BARROWS

CHAPTER 1

The Upright and the Uptight

How would you describe them?

"The beautiful people?"

"Dirty, long-haired, unwashed, good-for-nothing communist-inspired louts?"

"Peace-loving, socially responsible, politically aware members of society?"

"Rebellious, thankless, self-centered hooligans?"

"Sex-obsessed, pleasure-loving, work-shy, drug-addicted layabouts?"

"Dangerous, destructive anarchists?"

"Normal, healthy, red-blooded, hardworking kids?"

There are more of them than ever before.

Healthier because of the balance of their diets.

Wealthier because of the balance of payments.

They travel more

See more

earn more

spend more

demand more

receive more.

Publicized

Criticized

Idolized

Pressurized

Analyzed

Shouted at

Shot at

Spouted at
Spat at
They are pandered to,
    planned for,
    pleaded with and
    preached about.

Cheering, jeering
Swinging, singing
Learning, burning
Hippies, Yippies
Nudity, crudity
Turning on, putting on
Dropping out, making out
Pot, pop and pill
Hairy, scary
Drug scene
Teen scene
Obscene
The whirling world of YOUTH.

Meanwhile back at the Church . . .
Preachers preach
Sermons carefully, prayerfully prepared.
Expositional
Exegetical
Dispensational
Devotional
Inspirational
Indigestible.
Information leads to
Illustration leads to
Invitation leads to
Integration into
Congregation.
        (Membership is increased.)
Deacons deac.
Business-like and Christ-like men
Running a well-oiled operation.
Budget met

Baptistry wet
Regularly.

> (Membership is satisfied.)

Tithers tithe
Large tenths in tiny envelopes.
Faithfully, cheerfully giving
abundantly out of abundance
Ensuring

> (Membership is comfortable.)

Choristers chorus
Impeccably gowned and groomed
With an excess of crescendos and sopranos
Rousing, rising anthems.

> (Membership is inspired.)

Well dressed
Well pressed
Well blessed

> (Membership is dismissed.)

The placid world of CHURCH.

Two worlds on one planet.
The woolly weird Youth World.

> The calm, cool Church World.

The weak and wild world.

> The meek and mild world.

The rebelling, revolting world.

> The redeemed, respectable world.

The "out of sight" world.

> The "out of touch" world.

And never the two shall meet . . .
But they must!

CHAPTER 2

Pot, M*A*S*H* and Ostriches

There was a time when dope was a glue used by model airplane enthusiasts.

And a pot was the receptacle in which the dope was kept.

A groove was the slit where the dope from the pot was poured.

And a joint was made by fitting another piece of wood into the groove.

Great care was taken to insure that the joint was square.

But not any more!

Now dope means drugs.

Pot is marijuana.

To groove is to be part of the drug scene.

And a joint is marijuana ready for smoking.

A straight is someone who doesn't participate in the drug scene.

And he and his kin are called squares.

So unless you want to be severely misunderstood, don't say, "I must get some dope out of this pot and pour it into a groove so that I can fit these straight pieces of wood together and make a square joint." Because to a modern youngster you will be saying, "I must get some drugs out of this marijuana smoke ready for the reactionary Establishment." Hardly the most enlightened thing you ever said!

But don't run away with the idea that it is only a problem of semantics—that it is only the vocabulary that has changed, because you would be absolutely wrong. As far as modern youth is concerned, nearly everything has changed.

Not too long ago the average teenage boy (if there is such a creature!) was a clean-cut youth with straight back, healthy grin, white teeth and tux. He would have a date with a cute little girl with lips like Cupid's bows, eyebrows like his arrows, curls everywhere, dimples, ruffles, buttons and bows. They would go to a movie showing Errol Flynn kicking horrid little Japs out of Burma, drink a milk shake on the way home, talk about football and cheerleading for a few moments, and if all went well a chaste kiss at the door would send him on his way rejoicing and her to her room glowing.

But now it is not unusual to see a boy and girl with hair of equal length go to watch Elliot Gould sloshing through the blood of M*A*S*H, preaching the anti-war gospel, mocking the flag, debunking religion and sneering at marriage. She peers from darkened eyes through tinted glasses and masses of long straight hair. He seems half-stoned and disinterested, floating in a psychedelic world, giggling for no apparent reason, estranged and detached from the world around. They don't talk football and cheerleading because they both dropped out of school. They talk philosophy, astrology, revolution, the Panthers. And he doesn't get a chaste peck at the door of her apartment because in all probability it isn't hers, it's theirs! He doesn't leave rejoicing and she doesn't go to her room glowing. They live there. It's their pad.

The whole tone and tempo of modern youth has changed dramatically in the last few years. The speed of this change has left many older people gasping. "Older" means anyone over thirty years of age! Its revolutionary nature has reduced not a few to panic stations. And those who are not busy worrying themselves to an early grave about the young people are busy trying hard not to worry.

Of course, there is nothing either new or strange about worry and panic. Man has always been prone to panic when confronted with something unexpected, unwanted or unexplainable. And much of what the young people are doing and saying today falls into these categories.

13

One panic reaction is to run from the scene . . . nose down, heading for the horizon, stopping for nothing, shouting, "Follow me, men." Another reaction does just the opposite. It bunches its fists, gets red in the face and fights, shouting. "I don't like you, I don't understand you, you frighten me, threaten me, disturb me, and bug me so I must annihilate you."

A compromise between these two is also common. It is the ostrich reaction. The ostrich, when he sees what he doesn't want to see, has to convince himself that he hasn't seen what he knows perfectly well he has seen. So he sticks his head in the sand. As a result he can't see what he saw, and then happily evading his fears he rests his tiny brain in the warm softness of his self-induced ignorance.

None of these reactions to modern youth is of any lasting value. Why run from them when their numerical strength is so great that in a short time over half the population of the United States will be under twenty-one years of age? Young people are so numerous, so vocal, so alive that their impact will be felt in increasing measure in the next few years. Their attitudes are going to change things drastically. And not only for themselves, for everyone! It's no good running from them. They have arrived.

And why fight what you don't understand? You may even find yourself fighting something valid, hindering something progressive and blocking a development that time will prove to be the right one. There is always the possibility that the youngsters may not be only irresponsible and irrational and irreverent. There is the distinct possibility they may have something to contribute, something to say and something to which we ought to listen.

As far as the ostrich stance is concerned—that's for the birds! Because the only thing it ever did for a person was stiffen his neck and clog up his vision, and we can do without stiff-necked people without any vision in this situation.

CHAPTER 3

The Cat's Whisker

"The Cat's Whisker" is very precious to me. It is a small coffee house situated on the outskirts of Manchester, England. The young people of the area used to come there to drink coffee, listen to their music and grow their hair. There were so many of them that they filled the tables and chairs and the vacant areas and flooded onto the sidewalks in the hundreds. Just normal healthy kids with nothing much to do. From some of those young people in "The Cat's Whisker" I learned a big lesson for which I will be eternally grateful. Let me tell you how it all came about.

I didn't frequent coffee houses because that wasn't my environment, and my background didn't encourage me to go to that kind of place. I was raised in a Christian home, introduced to Christ at an early age and taught the Word of God as soon as I was teachable. My home was situated in a comfortable, healthy, vigorous environment. We had enough of everything and too much of nothing. School days were normal and at the end of them a bank opened its doors to offer me an inviting career. A clean-cut, secure, well preserved, thoroughly decent, middle class respectability lay ahead of me.

The Korean War intervened and the Royal Marines decided that I ought to join them in their efforts to beat whoever it was who was opposing us in Korea. I did nothing to help win the War because I showed some aptitude at playing Rugby football. So they put me on the Marine football team, and while I did nothing about the War, I did help the Marines to beat the Army at Rugby.

After two years, I returned to my banking career with an honorable discharge, a healthy commando-trained body, and a remarkable wound certificate stating that I had been wounded in active service in the Royal Marine Commandos in that I broke my nose playing Rugby for the Marines!

Years ticked by, and my career flourished, my preaching flourished, and my marriage flourished. Everything in the garden was flourishing.

Then something strangely uncomfortable began to get to me. On weekends I used to travel preaching the Gospel. Everytime I got home, Jill, my wife, would say to me, "Did you have a good weekend?"

"Yes, dear," I invariably replied.

"How many people were there?" was always the next question.

"Oh, a very nice number," I replied evasively.

"As many as that crowd over there?"—and she would point across the road to "The Cat's Whisker" where hundreds of young people would be standing around aimlessly. She bugged me about them, and they bugged me about themselves. I knew that I was busy preaching my heart out to people who knew the message as well as I did, while those kids who had no idea about it crowded my doorstep. And I did nothing to tell them about the Lord Jesus.

I became increasingly concerned about them, but I was unwilling to do anything about them. And the reason? I was scared of them! Funny enough, I wasn't scared when I was in the commandos. But I was scared of those kids! Sometime later I found out what I was scared of. A youth shouted out at me, "You preachers are all the same. You stand up in your pulpit six feet above contradiction, and you're scared to come down where we are!" And he was right. I was perfectly secure in a church with an oak pulpit and an orderly crowd sitting quietly in rows, but I didn't fancy my chances of mixing with a group of kids milling around on the sidewalk and starting to talk to them.

16

So I did what most Christians do. I went regularly to church and joined in the general criticism of the young people who never came to church. But I was uneasy about that, too. Because I didn't know why they weren't coming, and therefore, I wasn't in any position to talk intelligently on the subject.

Deep down I knew that I had no honest alternative but to go to them and stand on their sidewalk or sit in their coffee house and find out what made them tick and see if I had anything to offer them. So one night, I took a deep breath, prayed a fervent prayer, looked furtively over my shoulder to see if any Christians were watching and stepped into "The Cat's Whisker." It was full and dark and noisy and frightening. I felt like a whale at a garden party, big, obvious, floppy and useless. A little voice inside me said, "Run," and it took a lot of determination not to obey it!

Somehow or other I got into a conversation with a young man who wasn't exactly my type. Remember, I was a clean-cut ex-Marine with a banking career who preached in his spare time. My new friend was wild and woolly, shaggy and irreverent. But to my amazement, he was friendly, open, interested and intelligent. He kindly asked me what I was doing there. So I said something about being interested in helping young people. He was all in favor of that, and he asked me how I thought I could help. I hurriedly answered that I couldn't help but I represented Someone who could and eventually he got it out of me that I wanted to talk about Christ. "Great," he said, "let's get on with it!" You could have knocked me over with a feather! I certainly had not anticipated his interest, and I was completely thrown by his openness.

A long conversation ensued, and then he looked at me pointedly and asked, "Do you really believe all this?"

"Yes," I replied.

"Honest?" he said, with a trace of unbelief.

"I do," I assured him with added emphasis to denote fervor and conviction, "I do"—for good measure!

"I don't believe you," he said flatly.

I was insulted and flashed back, "Why don't you believe me?"

"Because," he said, "if you really believed what you say you believe, you would have been down here before tonight to tell us." And with that he gave me a contemptuous look, rose from the table, paid for his coffee—and left.

I was completely stunned and humiliated. More than that, I was put on the spot because I knew that there was a lot of truth in what he said. So I went home a very quiet and troubled young man; troubled because of the inconsistency of my profession. I believed that Christ died for all, but I didn't believe it enough to tell people; troubled about the brutal openness of the boy who had taken me apart; troubled because of my inability to handle him; troubled because he was open and interested, and I couldn't reach him; troubled because if the world was full of people like him, and the church was full of people like me, then we were in a mess.

That night was a turning point in my life. I told the Lord about the whole situation. He didn't learn a thing, but I knew He was glad that I was learning. I also told Him that I was scared of these young people, but I really wanted to get to them. I wanted to reach the vast crowds of young people whom the church was not reaching. I honestly wanted to start caring for the young people for whom it appeared to me that the church did not care enough.

Many men of God have been of great help to me in my spiritual life, but so was my long-haired friend in "The Cat's Whisker" whose name I never knew and whom I would not recognize if I saw him again. That night he taught me many things. Let me list them for you.

He taught me that:

1. Modern kids aren't as fierce as they sometimes appear.

2. Many a keen mind operates behind a shaggy beard.

3. Modern kids are thinking more deeply than I did at their age.

4. They are more reachable than most Christians want to believe.

5. I had nothing personally to offer him at that time.

6. I had better shape up and quick!

Since that time, I have been less apt to criticize the young people of today and more anxious to understand them. I have become considerably less antagonistic toward them and more concerned for them. Instead of being repelled, I have been drawn to them. In fact, the more I get to know them, the more I find a crushing burden for them.

It takes time, patience, tolerance, insight and exposure. It hurts and it costs and it challenges. It alters your thinking; it changes your outlook; it shifts your approach. In fact, when you start to get to the exploding youth of today, they start to get to you. So, if you don't want this to happen, please don't read any more. Give this book to a friend!

CHAPTER 4

Grass, Speed and Peer Fear

Not long ago, a man came to talk to me about some young people with whom I was working. He said that he felt they had to be kept away from the "decent" young people, and he wanted me to understand his position. I told him that I understood his position perfectly because I had met people like him before, people who arrive at conclusions and engage in actions based on fear or prejudice or both.

When it comes to dealing with today's young people, fear and prejudice are rampant in the church. Many people know it, admit it, hate it, but don't know what to do about it. "Perfect love casts out fear"—and that is the answer to the fear problem . . . and deeper understanding casts out prejudice. I'm quite convinced of this, but the church needs a tremendous flood of Holy Spirit love to cast out the fear and an outsized dose of down-to-earth common sense and insight to purge the prejudice.

The work of the Spirit of God in all His fullness in the Christian's life is intended and designed to flood that individual with the love of God. And His kind of love can swamp any fear. I have written two books on this subject, *The Fullness of Christ* and *Living Dangerously*. I don't intend to deal further with this side of things at this point, for I believe that the spiritual principles I tried to outline in those books will lead people to an experience of the fullness of the Spirit which in turn will shed the love of God abroad in their hearts in a lovely way. This will deal with the fear they will quite naturally have for the young people whom they do not understand.

On the other hand, I believe that a lot of solid thinking needs to be done by Christians today to deal with the problem of prejudice against the young person. We need to take time to look into the whole youth situation, understand it, and see what can be done about it. Let's try it and see what happens.

The youth scene and spotty faces have something in common! They are both covered with minor eruptions. It doesn't matter where you look either, on the youth scene or the spotty face. You'll see something bursting out all over, and sometimes the things that are bursting out are not pleasant.

People's reactions to both are similar, too. There are those who look on both and say, "Yuk." And others who look at both very carefully, examine them and say, "How interesting, I wonder what is causing this!" It's the second approach I long to see taken by many Christians toward today's young people.

A doctor approaches a spotty face, looks at it, carefully noting the symptoms, diagnosing the condition, suggesting an antidote and commencing the treatment. This must be done by today's church.

Let me suggest to you some of the eruptions I have seen in recent years in the youth scene. They are not listed in any particular order, and the list is not intended to be exhaustive. I think you will probably agree that all the things I am going to list are to be seen in greater or lesser measure wherever young people are to be found.

1. Drugs
2. Sex
3. Fashion
4. Music
5. Revolution
6. Mysticism
7. Communal living

Drugs

The Chinese have been smoking opium for centuries, and no one in the Western world worried about that.

The American Indians have been on peyote to help them in their religious activities and that was fine, too. Business men have been on the "pep-you-up-in-the-morning" and "slow-you-down-in-the-evening" kick for some time and that was perfectly permissible. Mom got on the cocktail and nicotine thing because of her neurotic stresses—and that was socially acceptable. Then rumors began to circulate about athletes being doped, and that was regarded as being all in the game. Nasty rumors about some pop stars using dope were disbelieved, because no one wanted to believe them, and then the whole thing exploded.

Dr. Timothy Leary began to preach the drug gospel and left Harvard in a hurry. The Beatles and the Rolling Stones sang songs alluding to drugs which went over most of our heads. Marilyn Monroe died from an overdose. A top politician resigned mysteriously with hints of drug addiction hanging thick in the air. Hippies preferred pot to nicotine and smoked in their contemplative circles. Actors were arrested at airports for having drugs in their baggage, and most of them claimed that they were framed. Movies began to depict "acid trips." Newspapermen wrote heart-broken articles about the chagrin with which they discovered that their children were on dope. The daughter of a TV personality took a trip and fell to her death. Radio, TV, movies and newspapers began to scream the message, "Drugs are big."

But it took people a long time to realize how big. School authorities denied that there was any problem in their area until they were proven wrong. Suburbia admitted that the ghettos had a drug problem, but suburbia didn't, until doctors' daughters were arrested in the homes of wealthy dentists having pot parties. Slowly and reluctantly decent, middle-class people began to admit the awful truth that the drug scene was big, and that their kids were involved. Back of all these reluctant people came the church members who really just didn't want to know what it was all about.

Dave Wilkerson had written *The Cross and The Switch Blade* and it was read widely by the saints with much clucking of evangelical tongues and prayers of "Lord, deliver us." But mainly the church thought that this was a "way out thing" confined to some rather unsavory areas of New York and accordingly she was singularly unprepared to cope with the problem—and in many instances still is!

But anyone who knows anything about young people —and is honest—admits that the drug problem is so big now that it is even reaching down to youngsters in junior high schools and may even be in some grade schools. One kid, twelve years of age, died recently— a heroin addict!

"Why," many people ask, "would any kid in his right mind ever start taking drugs knowing the possibility of addiction, the horrors of withdrawal, the danger of infection, and all the other things to which he may be laying himself open?" The answer—for the same reason that his parents go in for nicotine and alcohol knowing the same things!

I remember flying back from Jamaica to New York some time ago. A fashionable lady was sitting next to me, and she chain-smoked from the moment we took off to the time we began to circle New York for two hours waiting for our turn to land. She was obviously very agitated, and I got into a conversation with her. She told me that she was very worried about her teen-age daughters whom she had left in New York. The cause of her worry was that she didn't trust them, and she felt they might be having a pot party while she was away.

I sympathized with her concern. But I also pointed out to her that, in the eyes of her daughters, she was "hooked" on nicotine which has been proven addictive and deadly dangerous while denying them the right to smoke pot which has not, as yet, been proven addictive or dangerous.

23

The lady was having problems seeing that in actual fact she was probably one of the basic causes of her youngsters taking pot, but she also couldn't see that the youngsters were doing it in a modern genre to preserve the differential between the "youngsters" and the "oldsters" which they feel is so important.

But what are the reasons for the youngsters going in for drugs? I believe that one major reason is fear—that strange and frightening pressure to which people in every stratum of society and at every age level are subjected. "Everyone's doing it, and if I don't, they'll think I'm stupid," is expressed by many people to rationalize their reasons for wanting to engage in some activity. Many people can testify to the fact that they have been presented with the awful ultimatum, "If you don't try it, you're chicken."

The problem of "peer" fear among young people is accentuated by the determined effort of pushers to involve more and more in the habit to finance their own drug-taking. In these many instances the fears are real and justified. I have met young people who have been so physically threatened by unscrupulous youths that they have been more afraid to refuse the drugs than they have been to accept them and start using them.

Then, of course, there is the old "stolen apples are sweetest" idea. "The grass on the other side of the fence is always greener." Anything that is forbidden must be worth trying, or it wouldn't be worth forbidding it! When I was a kid, this was excitingly true. Smoking was forbidden to me, so one lovely afternoon I went to the back of the greenhouse with my friends, rolled some dried tea leaves in a piece of newspaper, tried smoking it and was gloriously ill. That was the end of my smoking career. The only reason I wanted to try the whole business was that I had been told I shouldn't.

When I was in the jungles of South America, I saw the same kind of thing. The Indians never build walls on their houses, and when the missionaries did, the

Indians assumed there must be something they wanted to hide, so they poked holes in the walls and became insatiable "Peeping Toms." The idea being, of course, that if it was forbidden, it must be worth seeing, and if it was worth seeing, it was worth poking holes to see it.

I suppose that most kids have to get their adolescent kicks somewhere (and the tragedy of today is that the drug kick is involved). The adventure of dabbling in the forbidden is a great attraction to any youngster with red blood in his veins, particularly if his parents are against it. Some young people have said that the only time their parents ever showed any interest or concern for them was when they got on drugs. I feel that they are pushing their point a little, but maybe they have something here. Others have told me quite definitely that they started on drugs to get even with parents whom they felt had failed in their parental role. There's no doubt that many parents have failed and that many of their kids are bitter. Equally there is no doubt that a youngster can really hit his parents where it hurts most by getting into the drug scene because there is still social stigma attached even in our permissive middle class society.

There is another interesting thought pattern behind the drug scene. Young people are incorrigibly idealistic and their idealism is often at odds with what they consider to be the hypocrisies of the older generation. They shout loud and often against anything "unfair." One of their big gripes is that the adult society has decreed that pot, which has not been proven addictive, is illegal, while alcohol and nicotine, which have been proven addictive, are perfectly legal. One tends to sympathize with their disgust without condoning their actions in articulating their disgust. In fact, many kids feel that by engaging in the dope scene they are campaigning against the hypocrisies of a corrupt adult society and are becoming the champions of honesty and integrity. They certainly engaged in quite a bit of perverted rationalization to arrive at that conclusion, but I guess most of us have engaged in this particular kind of inverted righteousness at one time or another.

But to my mind, there is a bigger factor involved than any I have just outlined. There is a certain drug philosophy which has been peddled and portrayed by glamorous over-publicized people. This has captured our kids. They have been told that dope offers new perspectives: expand your mind—deepen your consciousness—lift you out of the mundane—transport you into undreamed-of realms. "Drugs," they have been told, "can make a note of music take on an infinite variation of tone." "Flowers become glorious in a thousand ways, colors take on new meanings, the total man is deepened and enriched and entranced." "You may even see GOD!"

This sounds great and exciting. It has been called educational . . . transcendental. It has been preached as being a means of religious experience. And many young people have swallowed the whole bit—hook, line and sinker.

They have been taught that when they have an exam they should pop a pep pill. When they are worried, they should take a tranquilizer. They have been introduced to a life of chemical adequacy—synthetic sufficiency—instant release—and capsuled euphoria. It's all heady and exciting, and very dangerous.

Of course, they have their fears. They fear losing control of their rational capabilities. They fear that their behavior under drugs may alienate them from their contemporaries. Some of them even fear the possibility of discovering under drugs the truth about themselves, and others fear that if they do discover a new wonderful world on a trip that they will never want to return to the rational world which has brought them so much disillusionment. They may go too high to want to come down again.

Many older people are convinced that the youthful use of drugs is totally irresponsible, but I don't think that I agree altogether. There is something more than irresponsibility involved. It is the willingness to take a calculated gamble. I know that many young people on drugs are just being silly, stupid and irresponsible, but others have thought deeply about the whole situation and are prepared to risk it.

But why would young people take this kind of gamble and consider it worth trying? Simply because they figure the possibilities of enlargement and discovery are so great anything would be worth trying to gain them.

Timothy Leary, the high priest of the drug scene, taught many young people that the risk of rational disorder is worth taking compared to the possibility of rational expansion. The kids felt that the possibility of a horrific bad trip was worth risking in the light of the possibility of a euphoric experience.

In other words, young people have a yawning vacuum of experience that they will try anything to fill. Knowing the risks, they'll take the drugs. Understanding the dangers, they'll go into it with their eyes open, longing and hoping and yearning for something to fill up that which is a vacuum in their lives.

I believe the fixation on drugs in modern young people is symptomatic of a search for adequacy, a search for meaning, and a search for fulfillment. And if that is the case, then modern youth is shouting out loud and clear the message which I believe with all my heart. This message is that man can only be adequate and have meaning and find fulfillment when he abandons his life to an all-sufficient Christ. That's where the church comes in.

Instead of being repelled and embarrassed, the church must recognize that the drug phenomenon is unmistakable evidence of a great yearning, a frightening search on the part of thousands of young people. They are searching for Christ whom the church professes to represent. Don't look at the drugs and say, "Yuk." Look at them and say, "How interesting," and then come up with an answer for the situation and start the treatment!

27

CHAPTER 5

Infection, Detection and Conception

Sex

The father of a pretty senior high school girl was worried. "When I was getting ready for college, it was an exciting time for my whole family. But we aren't getting excited about our daughter, Cindy, going to college—we're dreading it! She's going to be exposed to pressure on every hand—intellectually, socially and morally. And it's the morals that worry us most," he said. "She's a good girl. She's never given her mother and me any trouble, but how will she cope with all the immorality she will encounter?"

In all probability, Cindy is not as naive or as unversed in the phenomenon of the sexual revolution as her dad thinks. Indeed, it is hard to see how she could be unaware of what is really happening, however sheltered her life at home has been. The sexual revolution has by no means been confined to the college campus, for like the drug revolution, it has invaded the high school and junior high school environment.

It is common knowledge that the instance of venereal disease among young people has assumed what some medical authorities call "epidemic proportions." High school authorities have been forced to make special arrangements for pregnant students. Youngsters are maturing physically and sexually earlier in life, and their knowledge has kept pace with their development.

Talking to teenagers today can be quite an experience. They have their own specific sexual terminology which they use openly to relate both their sexual fantasies and experiments. As a result, any well meaning adult may find himself in a veritable minefield of double and triple meanings as he talks to them. I have certainly had some of my well meaning talks exploded as I have inadvertently used terms which caused the kids great amusement. They are perfectly free and open in their articulation and give no evidence of any restraint whatever in their conversation concerning sexual matters.

Their knowledge of sexual norms and sexual deviations is often much greater than that of their parents. The age of sexual innocence, or whatever you want to call it, has gone forever. What most of these young people don't know now about sex, they probably will never know. They discuss the pill among themselves in the same way that their mothers discussed cookery. They debate their conquests now in the locker rooms whereas their dads in their day had to talk about "conquests" that were little more than the products of an overfertile imagination.

One pretty little teenage girl told me recently that a certain person whom we were discussing was a "fag." She said it with calm conviction and was perfectly unembarrassed about it despite the fact that she had only met the gentleman a few hours previously. Her observations were acute. Her articulation was blunt. Her candor was brutal. But when it comes to sex, that's how it is right now.

When Cindy arrives in college, she will be told immediately where she can obtain her contraceptives. She will meet fellow students who will live together out of wedlock. There will be opportunity for her to live in co-educational domitory blocks and she will have no shortage of opportunities to demonstrate or develop her sexual prowess, as the case may be. Premarital sex will be common. Her virginity—or otherwise—will be an early topic of conversation, and Cindy will know that her campus is a veritable Mecca for sexual enthusiasts.

If Cindy had been born in an earlier generation, she would have been told little or nothing about sex. However, she would have learned that sex outside marriage is wrong and that she should "save herself" for the boy whom she would eventually marry. Should she be tempted to experiment with sex, she would be presented with three arguments against it in the form of deterrents.

The first has been described as the "fear of infection." She would be told that premarital sex would probably result in her contracting what was rather euphemistically called "a social disease." Secondly, there was the "fear of conception" or, in other words, she would be told that if she engaged in premarital sex she might get pregnant and bring shame on herself and her family. And in all probability this would ruin her scholastic career and also be responsible for bringing an unwanted child into the world. Thirdly, she would be told about the "fear of detection." Just imagine if she and her boyfriend were to be discovered engaging in the sexual relations—what a stigma this would bring upon her! What would everyone think!

Despite what we may think of the pros and cons of the three deterrents, there is little doubt that they did deter. But they also produced the necessity for specific answers to the age-old question, "How far can you go?" Such terms as necking, petting, and heavy petting came into being, and timetables were stipulated for gradually increasing intimacies, necking while going steady, petting when wearing his pin and/or ring, heavy petting during engagements, etc.

Then came the revolution, and *bang* went the three deterrents. The fear of infection no longer seemed to frighten them, as is quite obvious from the vastly increased number of young people suffering from venereal disease. Young people were told that drugs would be available to cure the disease, and they were no longer told that there could be serious consequences for those people who contracted these diseases. Well meaning authorities made it possible for youngsters to get treatment privately without even their parents knowing. A quick, painless, hushed-up cure for the unfortunate took the sting out of the fear of infection.

The much publicized pill arrived. It's very title—*"the pill"*—put it in the forefront of the thinking of both young and old alike. Until that time there had been pills and pills, but now *"the* pill"—wow—*"the* pill," the passport to "the experience" had arrived, readily and cheaply available, easily and painlessly administered.

In many instances its use was encouraged by threatened mothers who, faced with the necessity of deciding between the possibility of a pregnant daughter and the possibility of a promiscuous daughter, settled for the latter as the lesser of the two evils. Confidentially, at first, girls admitted to being "on the pill." But it wasn't long before the way-out swingers were busy preaching it and thereby issuing an unmistakable invitation. *Bang* went the fear of conception. Who feared pregnancy anymore? And if anything went wrong, abortion was the "in thing." But if you didn't want an abortion, then, of course, there were plenty of well-known people who were having children out of wedlock, and no one seemed to mind anymore.

And the fear of detection? Times and trends have changed so radically and so quickly that the fear of detection was superseded by the fear of derision. No longer were people afraid that others might know that they were engaging in sexual activity, but rather they began to fear people might know they were *not* engaging.

Some time ago a young student came to talk to my wife and me about something which was deeply troubling her. She wanted to know if we regarded her as being normal. The reason this young lady was inquiring about her sexual normality or abnormality was this: she had let it be known that she had not engaged in any sexual relationship with a member of the opposite sex. Her fellow students immediately assumed that the only person in her age bracket who had not engaged in heterosexual activity must be homosexual, and they had told her so. Because the situation now is so hopelessly out of control, many young people regard heterosexual activities outside of marriage as perfectly permissible. They also regard homosexual activities as normal, and the only thing they will not tolerate is the attitude that denies the right to engage in sexual activity outside of marriage. The situation is extremely serious.

But how did it all happen? And why did it happen? One thing must be said loud and clear. Present-day young people are not wholly responsible for the sex scene as it is. They do not publish *Playboy* and *Penthouse*. They do not hold the purse strings of Madison Avenue which blatantly and cynically uses sex to boost sales. They did not put suggestive advertisements on television to sell shaving cream and hair rinses. They did not open the topless, bottomless and everything else-less joints that proliferate downtown in most cities. They didn't rationalize the pornography laws until pornography was readily available at every airport and drugstore. Their dads did this.

Today's kids did not instigate the stag movies and bring it to the wide screen of the drive-in theater. They didn't invent mistresses on expense accounts and call girls at conventions. Neither did they engage in extramarital affairs and adulterous associations and the like which led to divorce proceedings and wrecked their homes and their families. But many of them were raised in an atmosphere in which these actions were accepted as normal.

They began to call it hypocritical to have one standard for dad and another for mom. They began to despise parents who said one thing about teenagers' sex life and did another thing on their own. They became annoyed with what they considered the abuse of sex in advertising and big business, and in the end they decided to reject the whole philosophy of sex that they had been taught by their parents. The girls found themselves emancipated, and, armed with the pill, they decided that what was good for the goose was good for the gander. They further decided that there was no point in being secretive about it. If it was enjoyable it was permissible. And they began to have fun. They flatly rejected what they regarded as a cynical, hypocritical, commercialized middle-aged approach to sex. They dragged the whole scene into the open and fornicated and could care less who knew.

It would be wrong to call it all promiscuity or animal behavior. I have talked with many young people who are products of previous mixed-up generations, and they have rejected the phony double standard they saw in their elders. They saw their hang-ups and hypocrisy and have been introduced to the heady philosophy of hedonism. They assured me that they were looking for *real* love, and they had a deep desire to understand the intricacies of the intimacies that were available to them through sex.

Some of them have told me of the battles their parents had at home. They shared with me the trauma of divorce proceedings and the turmoil as mom and dad struggled for possession of the kids. They knew what it was like to be pawns in the vicious fight between parents who had once professed love but later portrayed hate. They have decided that if that is what marriage does for you, the best thing to do is forget it and simply find someone with whom you are emotionally and physically compatible and live with them, provided it feels good for as long as it feels good. Sex without guilt. Relationships without legal straitjackets. Just love and freedom! That's what these kids tell me they are looking for.

Divine standards are being ignored. Moral standards are being changed. Sexual standards are being completely overhauled. And in the middle of all this upheaval stand millions of young people. No more wicked than their parents, and in all probability no more promiscuous than their fathers and their uncles were when they were soldiers and sailors in World

War Two, they are simply youngsters looking for satisfaction without subjection and love that will not lead to hate.

When I first realized that the sexual revolution—among other things—is evidence of a search for real love and real satisfaction and a rejection of phoniness and shallowness, I began to look at it in a different light. Because the revolution rejected Biblical principles, it was wrong and undoubtedly the "sincere search" of many people would lead only to disaster. Nevertheless, I saw the longing for a real enrichment that only true love and real commitment can bring. My heart began to leap and yearn for these youngsters, because for years I have been telling people about a Christ who alone can bring real love and deep lasting satisfaction. The sweetness that they are searching for is available in the Lord Jesus Christ. My attitude toward the young people who are engaging, for a variety of reasons, in the sexual license of the present day is one of deep concern coupled with a deep conviction that the Lord Jesus can meet the needs that their lives are betraying.

I deplore the abuses of sex among young and old alike. I hate the desecration of the sacred bond of marriage. I detest the intolerable pressures that are placed upon our young people by a sex-mad society. But I'm glad that all these things remind me that the world in which I live is full of young people looking for the love which my Lord alone can give.

CHAPTER 6

The Beatles, the Stones and the Rev. John Newton

Music

I was standing on a street corner talking to a boy one day, and I asked him what his plans were. He said, "My pals and I want to be like the Beatles."

"The what?" I inquired.

"The Beatles, you know, from the Cavern."

"Sorry," I replied, "but I have no idea what you are talking about. The Beatles, the Cavern—never heard of them." Patiently, he began to explain to me that a new pop group had arisen on the music scene called "the Beatles." He said they came from a part of Liverpool (which I knew well) called Bootle, and their music had a very distinctive beat, so they had put "Beat" and "Bootle" together and had come up with "Beatles." Even though I had not heard of the Beatles, I had some faint recollection of having heard of the Cavern, a remarkably small, dark and rather dingy cellar in the heart of Liverpool that had been converted into a dive where kids could hear their music and while away their hours.

My ignorance of the Beatles did not last long. Soon everyone was talking about them. Their pictures appeared everywhere. Four impudent-faced Liverpool kids with hair that was shockingly long!

(In a few years their original haircuts were to be like Yul Brynner's in comparison.) Their lively songs with a heavy beat began to be whistled and hummed. Young people of all ages began to watch them on "Top of the Pops." True, some of their words were slightly strange—they didn't make too much sense—but the tunes were fresh and fun.

Then nasty rumors began to circulate about the nice bunch of boys being somewhat less than lily white. But no one wanted to believe it, so no one believed it. Further rumors had it that some of the words that we didn't understand were hip words that had to do with drugs. Then some people said the Beatles were actually living on drugs. But no one wanted to believe that either.

They went to America and had instant success. Crowds of kids raved over their music and rioted at their shows. Then formal dinners at the British Embassies followed and the Beatles had arrived. Their return to England was broadcast on the BBC. One rather pompous interviewer asked Ringo Starr, "How did you find America, Mr. Starr?" "Oh, we went up to Iceland, and it was the first on the left," he replied. Everyone laughed and happily forgot the nasty rumors.

Bill Haley and the Comets had started something called "Rock and Roll." Elvis the Pelvis had followed up with his oily hairdo and his well oiled hips. Those in the know said it was all a development of Dixieland and progressive jazz, and those who weren't in the know either liked it or hated it. The kids were certainly going wild about it all.

Record sales began to soar. A new breed of cat called "disc jockey" began to appear. Programs specifically tailored for the young people came along. Soon it was difficult to get any other kind of music on the radio. Groups began to proliferate—The Rolling Stones, The Pretty Things—their music got wilder. Their hair got wilder. Their clothes got wilder. Everything became wilder and wilder!

Robert Allen Zimmerman started to write songs. No one has heard of Robert Allen Zimmerman, but everybody has heard of Bob Dylan. Zimmerman greatly admired the Welsh poet, Dylan Thomas, who died prematurely. In Dylan's memory, Zimmerman changed his name to Bob Dylan. His songs were quieter and folksy—played to a clever acoustic guitar background. His songs seemed to portray a lot of thinking on the part of the author and a lot of skill on the part of the performer. He seemed to be having problems about many things and to be protesting about most things. He made scathing comments about the Viet Nam War. He turned his keen eye and sharp wit on many other subjects. As a result of his leadership social comment became more and more evident in the songs to which the young people listened.

Singers and groups began to voice their protest more vehemently. Their philosophies came over with increasing clarity. They were advocating love and peace. "Make love, not war," became their theme. They preached drugs. They preached sex. The dances which their music inspired were little more than writhing actions with clear sexual connotations. Eyes closed, heads back, lost in a euphoric grinding, the kids danced away the hours.

In case this may sound like a middle-aged interpretation, let me remind you that a spokesman for the Rolling Stones said so that we could all understand, "Rock is Sex, and you'd better believe it."

Flashing lights, unrestrained gyrations, thinly veiled obscenities, double and triple meanings in the lyrics, decibels by the thousands began to develop, and the term "acid rock" appeared. Baba Ram Dass, formerly Dr. Richard Alpert, a colleague of Timothy Leary, in his Harvard days said, "I would say that ninety percent of the rock industry which is shaping the minds of the young today in a very dramatic way has been linked to acid."

Songs like "Tambourine Man," "Flying High," "The Crystal Ship," and many, many others became more explicit, and it became more apparent to all that the music world was firmly in the grip of the drug, sex circle, and the kids were being "taken in" again.

Some big names in the music world were busted.

Then in rapid succession, Janice Joplin and Jimmy Hendricks died from drug overdoses. Scandal followed scandal. Crooked disc jockeys were exposed for pushing discs in return for favors. Charts were rigged. And the music went round and round.

Yet at the same time another remarkable thing began to happen. The uninhibited songs speaking of the wild liberty of psychedelic experience gave way to some quiet, introspective, haunting melodies. The message switched to alienation, dissatisfaction and a searching for something real. Religious thought appeared in such lovely songs as "Bridge Over Troubled Waters." George Harrison of the Beatles wrote, "My Sweet Lord," a song professing, "I really want to know You." True, his theology wasn't as impressive as his music, for he got confused with Krishna toward the end of the song, but at least kids were singing about the possibility of knowing the Lord.

Then without any warning, "Jesus Christ Superstar" hit the market. With little or no conception of the deity of Christ and majoring almost completely on His humanity, the record-breaking musical appeared everywhere and its songs were on the lips of everyone however remotely connected with the music of today.

John Newton lived a wild life. At one time he was a slave trader and ship's captain. Eventually he became an Anglican rector. In all his wild life and in all his wildest dreams I don't suppose John Newton ever imagined that his lovely hymn, "Amazing Grace," would ever make the charts in 1970. But thanks to the rendering of Judy Collins, it did. Known by Christians around the world and sung for generations as a hymn of praise and worship, "Amazing Grace" suddenly became the theme of the youth masses.

Debates about "irreligious revival" or "hard-nosed irreverent businessmen" took the floor. As yet it is too early to come up with any answers, but there is no doubt that the twisting road of pop has at last taken another fascinating turn, even if no one knows where it is going next. More kids are singing and more kids are listening and more kids are writing and more kids are thinking than possibly ever before. The music scene certainly tells us this. And what they are singing and writing and thinking is of the utmost importance. I believe they are telling all who listen that they feel lost, that they are looking for something, that their search is so real they will try anything, that the things they have tried have failed, and now perhaps they are saying, "Maybe, Lord, You have the answer, and I really want to know You."

If that is the case, then I'm even more excited about the possibilities of singing the song of the Lord Jesus to these fascinating young people.

CHAPTER 7

The Long, the Short and the Hairy

Fashion

One day a seminar on youth that I was conducting for a group of pastors ran into trouble. Some of the men weren't too enthusiastic about my appraisal of the youth situation and the part that the church was playing in rectifying it. In exasperation, one of the pastors exploded, "Why do all these kids want to grow their hair so they look like mop heads?" I looked at him and his colleagues before answering. There was a full row of them wearing black suits, white shirts, gray ties. They were all overweight, and they all had crewcuts, and they just reminded me of a long black pod full of prickly black peas. "I don't know why they want to look like mop heads," I replied, "but I guess it's for the same reason that you all want to look like toothbrushes." That certainly didn't help my seminar one little bit either!

Mop heads or toothbrushes—which are right? Crewcuts or long hair, which is sacred and which is profane? Personally, I dislike both, but I crusade against neither.

"Hair" is not only the name of a rock musical, but it is also a topic of fervent debate. It has become a bone of perpetual contention, a symbol of philosophical ideology, and almost incidentally something that tends to grow out of people's heads. Longer locks and bushy beards and magnificent mustaches are here with a vengeance.

Of course, there is nothing new about long hair. A pastor who came with me into a coffee house in England asked a long-haired youth whom he met, "Why do you grow your hair like that?" The prompt reply, "I want to look like Jesus, that's why," shook my pastor friend rigid. Some saints don't like the idea of Jesus having long hair. Some have even written articles "proving" that He didn't, but whether His hair was long or not He certainly had hair on His cheeks because His tormentors tore it out. Elijah would have fitted right into a modern commune and never have been noticed. John the Baptist would have looked like one of the gang, and I guess Samson wouldn't have been too far away from looking like a hippie either.

A friend of mine who is the president of a very respectable Bible College in America was looking at pictures of the former Presidents of the United States of America. When asked why he was so interested, he said that he had been struck with how many of them had long hair, and he was trying to find out how many former Presidents were hippies!

Long hair has been worn by prophets preaching on the mountains and by Presidents presenting their inaugural addresses. It has been seen curling delicately beneath the helmets of football players and held back by multi-colored bands on the heads of seven-foot basketball stars. Hippies wear it, and artists wear it. Students tend their shoulder length locks and servicemen bundle their long hair under short wigs to meet the Army requirements. Long hair is very much a part of the scene.

Strangely enough, hair lengths and skirt lengths seem to be moving in inverse proportion to each other. The longer the hair the shorter the skirt! Mary Quant started something when she introduced the miniskirt. Previously only the guards stationed outside the Greek palaces had worn them, but the reaction of women all over the world showed that they had been waiting for the arrival of something like the mini. Many of them were so carried away that they went from mini to micro. More conservative girls huffed and puffed, but still took up their hems "just a little."

41

But the "rag trade" became alarmed. The mini needed less material and was getting too popular. So something had to be done. Something extreme enough to counter the mini and the micro. What could be better than the maxi? Men went on strike, women started to picket, maxi's got caught in elevator doors and on escalator steps. Entering and exiting from cars became an athletic exercise and the maxi-mini war was on. The midi tried to act as mediator but was dismissed by some as being "midi-evil," and the whole situation became so confused that in no time at all any length was accepted with equanimity.

Carnaby Street in swinging London was setting the pace. The fashion houses were trying to catch up. Moms weren't showing their daughters what to wear any more because the daughters were showing moms what to wear. Dress styles that were run up by hippie style kids one summer were selling on Fifth Avenue the next summer. For instance, they started the denim craze, and now would you believe that denim of all things is the top thing in all fashion houses!

Then came the ethnic thing. So the kids started to wear Indian headbands and African beads. Tassels and fringes, moccasins and leather became the thing. And mom dutifully followed just a few months in arrears!

Dads were having a hard time, too. Defenders of the clean cut, white shirt and necktie generation, they suddenly found themselves besieged by the "down with neckties" hoards. Beads took over. That's right! Beads! Pendants began to dangle from sweatshirts. Polo necks appeared with dinner jackets. Johnny Carson did it. Richard Burton did it. Lord Snowdon did it. The necktie, that antiquated symbol of neat respectability, was down. The end of the symbolic knot of frustrated manhood was in sight. Down and almost out! But not quite! Staging the biggest comeback of fashion history, the necktie returned bigger, broader, brighter and took its place alongside the beads, the bells, the pendants and any other thing that men had a notion to hang around their necks.

Long hair became so common that people with long hair weren't noticed anymore. So the skinheads arrived on the scene. John Lennon's much publicized wool was shorn and auctioned. Then he appeared blinking and bald in the public glare. Maxi's developed unbelievable splits. Hot pants arrived with a flourish of long, long legs.

Orange shirts with ruffles, purple pants with flares, shoulder bags with tassels became the dress of the "man about Manhattan." What on earth was going on! Whatever it was, the kids had started it off. Some folks protesting certain things took off everything and were duly photographed and reprimanded. Others took off everything, because it was the only fashion thing they could think of. They were photographed and left alone. The fashion scene was simply a scene where anything was permissible! And it still is—shouting loud and clear by what you wear and how you wear it, or what you don't wear and how you don't wear it, "Do your own thing." "Be your own man." "Don't conform." "Let it all hang out."

Fashion among young people has fluctuated wildly. It has fluctuated equally wildly among the older people but usually twelve months later. The more extreme it has been, the more popular it has become. From micro to maxi; from hot pants to pant suits; from shoulder length hair to skinheads! *Extreme* is the word.

Personally, I feel that in the very extremities of youthful fashion we have the best clue to what is really happening. In the happy-go-lucky atmosphere of "anything goes," it is becoming increasingly difficult to be noticed. The only hope of being noticed is to be extreme. If everyone is wearing a micro, a maxi is almost necessary. If everyone's hair is long, it is almost imperative to consider becoming a skinhead.

But why do so many people want to be noticed? I guess it's because everyone wants to be someone.

Everyone wants to belong. The bigger and brasher our world becomes, the harder it will be to be part of it. While everyone may not want to be the only pebble on the beach, at least they do want to be a pebble. And they want to be a pebble that is noticed.

I believe that while high fashion is being manipulated by the big business interests of Carnaby Street and Fifth Avenue many people are prepared to go along with this manipulation because, the way things are in the fashion world at the moment, they do at least have a chance of being noticed and to be something different.

A girl came into our church recently and was noticed! And that is putting it mildly! She wore a black, wide-brimmed hat covered with fluorescent felt flowers, an army greatcoat, blue jeans and sandals. On the seat of her blue jeans she had sewn a copy of the flag of the United States of America. I had occasion to counsel with her and was delighted to do so. She talked long and interestingly about her desire for a spiritual experience, and I enjoyed the time with her.

The following week another young lady dressed in a short, sharp dress, a tidy hairdo, and a generally neat appearance came to speak with me. She thanked me for the help I had given her, but I was a little embarrassed because I didn't even remember talking with her. Then she told me! She was the girl with the floppy hat and greatcoat and the flag bedecked jeans. But when she dressed in an unobtrusive way, she wasn't noticed anymore.

Neat, but anonymous! Subsequently, I discovered that she had desperately wanted to be noticed and wanted to be wanted. I think that this young lady is typical of many of the young people in the world today. They go for the most "way out" fashion they can possibly think of and by the very extremes of their appearance they are shouting, "Notice me." "I'm me, I want to be me." "I want you to acknowledge me as me."

And if that is what the modern kids want, then I certainly want to get to them and show them how they can be a real person and to show them how only God can make them the kind of person He created them to be. We're back to the same old thing—that the trends of these teens are trends that are symptomatic of a real spiritual longing and a deep spiritual search!

CHAPTER 8

The Generals, the Bishops and the President

Revolution

There is nothing new about rebellious teenagers. Ask any parents who have had some! Teenagers, I suppose, are strictly those people whose age includes the 'teen. In other words, a teenager is anyone from the age of thirteen to nineteen. Personally, I dislike the term because there is no comparison whatsoever between a thirteen-year-old and a nineteen-year-old. To all intents and purposes most thirteen-year-olds are children and most nineteen-year-olds are adults. However, if we may be permitted to generalize, I would say that teenagers are those members of the human race who are too old to be children and too inexperienced to be adults. Many of them have the body of a man and the attitude of a boy. Or they have the ideas of a woman and the pose of a girl. Teenage is a traumatic time of life.

Teenagers are a living battlefield torn apart inside by conflicts of mind and soul and body. They tend to get furious with the world and mad at themselves, frustrated by their parents and angered by their teachers or just plain embittered by their employers. Their attitude isn't helped by the fact that they are expected to behave maturely but are treated as if they were juveniles. Give them a gun—but refuse them the vote!

Just a few days ago I was talking with a youngster well over six-feet tall. He had a fine car which he had just wrecked. But he didn't seem particularly perturbed that, not only had he wrecked a very valuable piece of equipment, but he had miraculously escaped with his

46

life and, even more important, been saved from taking someone else's life. He is a very skillful driver, but he sometimes behaves as if he hasn't the remotest idea that the vehicle he is driving is more a lethal weapon than a means of locomotion. He drives with the skill of a racing driver and the mental ability of an idiot.

Teenagers are busy growing up and maturing. They are flexing their muscles. They are stretching their intellectual capacities. Their bodies grow and develop, and their idealism takes great strides. They use their parents and teachers like trampolines. Not necessarily to trample on, but to learn balance and adjustment. They have to achieve stability and mental and social agility that will launch them into life. And this is where parents and teachers come in.

Unfortunately some trampolines are not too enthusiastic about working on that happy blend of unrelenting tautness and easy yielding that a trampoline must have. Too tight and you break your neck as you hit the ceiling. Too slack and you break your neck as you hit the floor. It's this blend of tautness and yielding that is so hard to find, and many parents and other people in authority have been bounced on so hard that they have decided it just isn't worth the trouble.

Bouncing as hard and as high as they can, these young people are giving their trampolines a real hard time. They have demonstrated their bounce by way-out rebellion and by hammering on the adult door like any other youthful generation before them. But recent brands of young people have been bouncing higher and hammering harder, and twisted trampolines litter the landscape.

Parental abdication has not only cheated a lot of healthy young people of the opportunity to mature, but it has also put on the world market a generation of kids who have gotten away with murder. And now they are looking for more kinds of murder to get away with! Having obtained an unconditional surrender from their

47

parents, and having run their homes and their families, they are now turning their attention to their schools.

"Let's run our teacher like we run our parents. Let's have our school revolve around us like our home revolves around us. We made ridiculous demands at home, and our parents, rather than fight, delivered the goods. Let's present ridiculous demands at school and see what we can get away with. If they don't come up with our ridiculous demands, we'll present an unbelievable alternative, and if they won't come up with either then we'll lay down together and take concerted action." To call it mob rule and mass blackmail would be perhaps a little unkind but nevertheless it is not far from the mark.

Everyone knows that this is what many young people began to do. Berkeley campus became the scene of student demonstrations, sit-ins, teach-ins and what have you. Students took charge of administration buildings, sat in the president's office and smoked his cigars. They burned report cards and destroyed records. They fought with police and went happily to jail. Martyrs to their own cause!

Having a considerable amount of success in disrupting the work of the schools and colleges, they then turned their attention to the courts. They made determined efforts to turn the court proceedings into a circus. Intent on ridiculing the legal system, they taxed the judiciary to the limits. To a certain extent, they got their way. They took on the police. Confrontations developed. Tear gas began to fly. Baton charges, bricks and fire bombs followed each other with frightening escalation until one sad day a hail of bullets left some lovely kids dead on the Kent State Campus.

Students in Japan have been doing this sort of thing for years. Some South American universities were closed more than they were open. I remember being impressed with the quietness of the University of Panama when I was there until I noticed the whole thing

48

was boarded up and soldiers with machine guns were parading in the shadows.

The French students went one better. Having closed the Sorbonne they decided to bring down the government. And with the help of Danny the Red they almost did.

Family authorities, school authorities, legal authorities, political authorities—all came under attack. Just so long as it was authority!

Institutions like the church and the army naturally came in for the same kind of treatment. Bishops and generals were treated as jokes while the President of the United States was actually used as a target when he and his car were stoned. Draft cards were burned, flags were torn up. Nothing was sacred, and it almost seemed some of these young people felt that anything was permissible. Normal youth rebelliousness had become a revolution of alarming proportions.

Authority or anything that reeked of authority was like a red rag to a bull. Discipline became a dirty word, and large areas of the youth world began to stride over the hedges of restriction and break down the gates of authority leaving themselves free to cavort in the meadows of "freedom."

Or so they thought. They had been taught some of the teachings of Jean-Jacques Rousseau and his followers. Rousseau's philosophy was as simple as it was wrong. Man was born free and society trapped him. Man is basically good. Restrictions make him bad. To follow this through logically, the young people decided that the only way for man's inherent goodness to surface was to get rid of all kinds of restrictions. Families gave restrictions, schools gave restrictions, the law gave restrictions, and the government gave restrictions, so they had to get rid of all the restrictions so that the great goodness burning within the hearts of all the rising generation might come to the surface.

To fulfill their duty to a trapped humanity they felt they must rid man of his shackles and free him from his fetters. They must pitch the steel ball of society and the chain of authority in the lake of anarchy and be done with the whole sordid business of a society that has ruined man.

They began to dream of a state of anarchy in which glorious freedom dwelt. But the President and the police stood in the way. So the President became an ogre and the police became pigs. The law was a stumbling block and the church was a spoilsport. Marriage was a chain around people's throats, and schools were factories of lies and perpetuators of a society that was responsible for all man's ills.

One day I was talking to a group of young people on campus in California, and I asked them why they wanted to wreck the existing society and overthrow legally elected authority when they did not appear to have any valid alternative to put in its place. Their reply was interesting. "If you were on a runaway train and certain disaster lay on the track, what would you try and do?"

"Try and stop it, I guess."

"No, you wouldn't," they replied. "You would want to decide what you were going to do after you had stopped the train before you got around to stopping it, according to your way of thinking." I got their point!

They added, "You people of the Establishment (I was obviously thirty years of age plus) have no sense of urgency. Society is rotten. The military is hell-bent on blowing us all to pieces. The tycoons of business are busy polluting us to death. The Pope wants to fill the world with little Catholics and breed us to death. The politicians are playing God and letting half the world starve to death, and all you want to know is, what are we going to do. We don't know what we are going to do, but we're going to make sure that this rotten and stinking society of ours stops its headlong race to self-destruction. Maybe if we can stop that we can get around to thinking what we will put in its place."

The more I listened to these young people and many others like them, the more clearly I saw that the young revolutionary spirit that is so much a part of the 1970's is shouting that they want two things. They want to live and they want to be free.

I have no doubt that their definitions of both life and freedom would differ considerably from mine. Equally I have no doubt that their ways of achieving both would differ completely from my approach. But their desires and my desires are very similar, and this is my point of contact. If they want to find life, I want to show them how to find life. And if it's liberty they want, I know where it can be found. And it isn't in anarchy, because anarchy is a vicious, murderous thing. It simply allows every human being to do "that which is right in his own eyes."

And it never works either because the very person who demands that he should have the right to do what is right in his own eyes denies the other person the right to do what is right in his eyes. The remarkable inconsistencies of some of the young people who have been insisting on total freedom for themselves and yet in the very way that they have demanded it have denied others that freedom have been plain for all to see. If some of the youngsters had been prepared to see that their demonstrations were denying the freedom to study to their contemporaries, perhaps they might have approached things a little differently.

But having said that, I believe that there are many deep-thinking, earnest young people in many parts of the world who want life and freedom. They are the young people for whom the message of the Lord Jesus who said, "I am come that you might have life," is relevant. They are the people to whom Christ has something to offer when He says, "If the Son shall make you free, you shall be free indeed."

A British Cabinet Minister was speaking—or trying to speak—to a packed house at one of Britain's most famous universities. The event was being televised live

51

and the students knew it. They used the occasion to put on a highly organized demonstration against something or other.

The Minister's words were drowned continually. He was harassed, challenged, ridiculed and laughed to scorn. The chairman of the meeting became increasingly agitated, but the Minister remained perfectly calm and composed. The more unruly the proceedings became, the more unruffled he appeared.

Finally, he made himself heard and said, "When I was your age (hoots of laughter all around), I felt deeply, too. I demonstrated. I was an idealist. I abhorred injustice. I hated hypocrisy, but there the similarity between you and me ended. I went to Spain and *fought* in the Civil War for my deep convictions."

He was doing something that these young demonstrators hardly deserved. He was giving them the benefit of the doubt and assuming that their anger was genuine and their demonstration stemmed from idealism. Young people are incorrigible idealists and it is good that they are. The older they become, the more their ideals will be beset by difficulties. As time goes on, they will become realists, and many people think that a realist is simply a lapsed idealist who prostituted his ideals for considerations not always of the highest order. Black and white are the colors of youth. Gray and cream get into the spectrum with advancing years. And it would appear that black hates gray and cream infuriates white.

There's nothing new about demonstrations and sit-ins, although some of the young people act as if they have invented them. The Old Testament prophets did it. The Suffragettes did it.

But you must admit that modern young people have done it in a bigger and bolder way than their predecessors. Martin Luther King captured their imagination, and they marched with him to rectify the ills of the downtrodden black society. Black was black, and black was good.

52

Viet Nam was a Godsend to them. With increasing fervor and bitterness they began to demonstrate against the war that was dragging on interminably in Southeast Asia. In England they marched to Aldermaston and in the United States they marched on Washington. When Billy Graham invited the President to Knoxville, they chanted obscenities in unison. When the South African Cricket Team wanted to tour England, they protested until the tour was cancelled.

Homosexuals held protest marches in New York. Women's Liberation Front liberated their fronts and marched. Protests and demonstrations became the order of the day, and the children saw it so often on TV that they began to play "protests" instead of hospitals and mothers and fathers!

Some young people jumped on the bandwagon and used the protests as excuses for hooliganism. But many of them felt deeply and strongly just the same. Kids from secure homes spurned comfortable beds and sat out on the sidewalks. Some of them went to jail for civil disobedience. They took up the cudgels for a variety of causes, and social concern blossomed like the cherry trees in Washington, D.C.

There is no doubt that there was a sense of adventure involved in putting flowers in the muzzles of rifles of the National Guard and a feeling of well-being about rooting for the American Indians. Great fun was had in the camps of protestors and a great camaraderie sprang up among the participants. But it seems to me that there is more than the excitement and the camaraderie and the sense of righteousness involved. Let me tell you what I think it is.

I think that young people today are looking for a cause with which to identify. They need a common denominator around which they can gather—and protesting today's ills, real or imaginary, gives them just the meeting point they crave.

Radical in outlook and revolutionary by nature, they began to distress the Establishment and band together

53

to push for common objectives against the massive foe. Protests let them be heard and seen. And protests gave them a cause with which to identfy. Life for the affluent young in the affluent Western world had become a comfortable yawn and a self-centered drag. Protests became the in-thing, because it gave them a chance to do something—or at least shout about something.

And all this makes me very excited indeed. Because whenever I see a young person with the guts to rebel and the desire to identify and with a heart searching for a cause, I think I might have something to offer him. If they are prepared to suffer hardship and to take things to extreme ends, then I just love to tell them about a Lord Jesus who *is* the greatest cause for which any boy or girl could ever live.

And this cause is something which will go on after all the blacks have been accepted by the whites, and after the South Africans have played cricket in England and after all the American Indians have all that they have wished for and after the bombing has stopped in Viet Nam. This cause will go on after all other causes have faded into oblivion, because this cause is the cause that brings life to people for time and for eternity.

The cause of Christ demands all or nothing, and I believe that perhaps for the first time in many years young people are beginning to show that they believe in all or nothing causes and are prepared even to suffer ignominy and shame and discomfort to be identified.

I disagree strongly with many of the things they are saying. I reject flatly many of the philosophies they are believing. I repudiate strongly many of the actions they have taken. But the sentiments they express and the desires they portray interest me and exhilarate me more than I can possibly say. I believe they are looking for the Lord.

CHAPTER 9

Woodstock, Haight-Ashbury and Togetherness

Sir Thomas More had his tongue in his cheek when he wrote about Utopia. He was kidding when he described his "perfect" island where everything was ideal. The very name, Utopia, means "no place" . . . the non-existent land of Man's dreams. But why didn't someone tell the kids that Utopia just isn't? Maybe their parents didn't know! Maybe their well-meaning teachers didn't know!

Of course the politicians didn't help too much either. The "American Dream" has been around for some time. The "Great Society" has been due to materialize for a year or two. Always, just around the corner, that elusive land of delight and liberty has beckoned and tantalized . . . never quite reachable, never quite knowable!

Somewhere along the line the youngsters decided that Utopia, *their* Utopia, was a possibility. So with all the ardor and enthusiasm of youth they made their plans and founded their own free society. They couldn't quite come up with an island like the one in More's sixteenth century dream, so they settled for something considerably less—Haight Ashbury!

What magic those two words began to work in the minds of America's youth. A society of the young, for the young and by the young, founded on *Love,* fostered by *Peace* with *Liberty* and *Equality* and *Fraternity.* From far and near the youth of America grabbed their bedrolls, left their homes, dropped out of their schools and hit the road. By air, by foot, riding their bikes or thumbing a ride, their twentieth century exodus began

—and San Francisco was the promised land. When they arrived, they were accepted. No one asked any questions. No one made any demands. No one was watching. No one had to prove anything. The kids had the feeling they were just themselves and everyone was happy to let them be themselves.

They could "come and go" as they pleased. They could wear what they wished. There were no deadlines to be met, no grades to be maintained, no projects to complete and no points to be scored. No one cared about money. No one was trying to impress. "Things" didn't matter any more. Only people mattered. Easy alliances were formed. Old taboos were ignored. Barriers were down and spirits were up. No one was killing any one—and people were *beautiful*.

If they needed anything, they asked someone. If they had it, they would share it. If they didn't, no one thought them inferior. They panhandled to meet their needs and sold their art to the curious. But it was the "curious" (and their need of the curious to support them) who began to undermine their Utopia.

Tourists arrived by the thousands. They looked at hippies like kids look at giant pandas in the zoo.

"Look, Ethel, a real, live hippy."

"He's got nice eyes, hasn't he."

"He stinks, Ethel."

"Let's buy some of his beads, Elmer."

"And finance his *fornication?*"

"Oh, Elmer, your mind . . ."

Californians on vacation began to visit them. The Golden Gate and Alcatraz came out a poor third to Haight Ashbury. The sensation-seeking middle class, middle-aged Americans swamped the serenity and devoured the distinctiveness of the youthful dream. Old-fashioned greed reared its head. Individuals insisted on their rights to their own individualities. Dope clouded kids' thinking, and the Utopian state sank in a pool of blood when the killing started.

The Love children carried knives to protect themselves. The Peace people fought for their existence, and an old familiar scene began to develop. Just like everywhere else, people were hating and killing and lying and cheating. Some of the kids returned home with their parents who had roamed the streets looking for their lost children. Others decided that they had made mistakes but that the dream was attainable—so they headed for the hills.

Communes sprang up. Where everyone shared everything, and people returned to the simple life. They tilled the soil and planted the crops, scraping at the dirt and scratching out a living. They built simple homes and started families with varying degrees of propriety. The quiet life, the simple life, the life of love and peace was their goal.

Something else was happening. It began at Monterey in June 1967, when the first Rock Festival was born. Since that time it has been estimated that over three million kids have attended fifty similar events—Woodstock, Isle of Wight, Altamont and many more.

While local inhabitants objected and local police mobilized, the kids arrived by the hundreds of thousands. With the intentness of pilgrims bound for their Mecca, they headed to the festivals, and when they got there they squatted on the ground (if they could find any of it vacant) and listened to the beat and wail of the continuous procession of Rock talent provided for them. All day and all night the music went on. The crowds sat and listened with remarkable fortitude. They curled up where they were to snatch a few hours' sleep—and the music went round and round.

Stories hit the front pages—stories of all kinds of misbehavior, fighting, nudity, public indecency, but support for the young people came from the most unexpected quarters. The Chief of Police responsible for the area in which one Festival was held said that he had expected all kinds of trouble from the estimated quarter of a million kids, but they had caused him fewer headaches than a few thousand people who attended the local football games.

The Media muscled in, of course. While the organizers of Woodstock were losing an estimated million and a quarter dollars, a movie company was busy making an idealistic movie and very realistic money.

Nudity was there, to be sure. But some said that it was posed by the newspaper men. Misbehavior there was, naturally. But what would you expect with so many teenagers? There was sex and there was dope. There was teen life with all its attendant faults. But overriding it all, there was a sense of well-being and a desire for a genuine meaningful experience.

Joan Baez called it "togetherness." And she well may have been right. Because men of all ages have been looking for that. The desire for an end to estrangement and hostility runs deep in the human soul. The toughest nut will crack under the right kind of pressure, and the hardest heart will yield to love and understanding. The most estranged and antagonistic person will respond to interest and concern, once his suspicions have been allayed. And this was all part of the search of the kids in their attempts at togetherness.

"Unrealistic," you may be saying. And I would be inclined to agree. And as I agree I feel a sadness in my heart, a sadness that the thought of Man living with Man as God intended Man to live is what the rising generation wants and is also what they are not going to get—a sadness caused by the knowledge that these kids are looking for the things that Christian preachers have been preaching about for years. But they are looking in the wrong places. I feel a sadness that those of us who know the Source of love and the Author of peace and the meaning of truth have been unable to communicate more than concepts to these youngsters.

This came home to me very forcibly when I had a strange experience in New York a few months ago. I "happened" to bump into a young fellow about twenty years of age. He recognized me immediately, but I didn't remember him, which wasn't surprising because he had grown a fine set of whiskers since I had seen him!

The last time we had been together was in England where we had spent a considerable part of one summer working on a project. He was a good worker, a pleasant, helpful companion, intelligent, alert and extremely likeable. As we worked together we had many opportunities to talk and I learned that he came from a wealthy family. He told me he had everything he could wish for, everything that money could buy. We talked about Christ a lot, and he loved to discuss the Christian Gospel. But he never committed himself to Christ, and in a strange way I admired him for this. Because in that particular environment, it was harder not to make a commitment than it would have been to make one. But he said he wasn't ready. What he told me in New York intrigued me.

"Stuart," he said, "I know Christ is real to you and I know you tried everything to make Him real to me. But neither you nor your friends were able to do it for me. And I was sorry about that, because I wanted to have what you have. I was unhappy with my life, even though I had everything that I could wish for, but I want you to know that at last I have found the life I wanted." I could hardly wait to hear what he had found.

"I have left the family home," he went on, "and I have gone to live in a commune. We love each other. We share everything together. I matter to people now —not for what I've got, but for what I am. I'm wanted, needed, appreciated, and I have never been so happy in my life, for I have found peace and love and all the things that are real in life. I've found them at last."

If I hadn't known this boy so well I would have dismissed everything he said by retorting, "Impossible," but I did know the boy, and I do remember the earnestness with which he spoke. He was for real! Don't misunderstand what I am saying. I am not agreeing that he had found a final substitute for Christ. I believe there is no such substitute. But he had found a community in which he experienced the things he needed—to some degree. The saddest part of his story came a few days later when I received a message telling me he had blown his mind with an overdose of drugs.

This boy and his predecessors in Haight Ashbury, the three million kids at the Rock Festivals and the boys and girls scratching the soil in California and New Mexico and other far-flung points around the world have much in common. They are looking for that precious elusive thing we call "Brotherhood." That strange indefinable something that makes men of all conceivable differences become one in love! What a noble search! What a thrilling objective! What a condemnation of a materialistic, selfish world! What a slap in the face for many a parent and teacher, pastor and leader who talks love and doesn't deliver the goods —and what an opportunity to tell the kids where real love and real brotherhood are to be found—*in Christ!*

CHAPTER 10

"I Ching," Zen and Ouija Boards

Mysticism

Orientals have always puzzled Occidentals. Their calmness, passivity and apparent fatalism have been more than pragmatic Westerners can understand. "Inscrutable" is the word that we always fall back on when we have tried to figure them out, and the very use of the word is in itself an admission of defeat. "You can't understand them," is what we are really saying. "We don't have to try to understand them," is the usual feeling, and with that we let them go their meditative, contemplative way while we head off in our own hard-headed, pragmatic direction.

But the day has come when the Oriental mysticism cannot be totally ignored because it has arrived in the West. It's the kids again. They have taken up with the whole thing and mysticism is their "bag."

The Beatles in their heyday surprised the world (or the part of it that was still able to be surprised by them) by taking off to India. There they sat at the feet of their favorite guru. Pictures of him clad in full length white robes, hairy and garlanded, surrounded by the Beatles similarly dressed appeared in all the magazines.

Jane Fonda, the darling of youthful activists, made the pilgrimage. Mia Farrow, after the breakdown of her marriage to Frank Sinatra, headed East. It was the "in thing" to have your own guru to go with your own doctor and your own hairdresser.

The Beatles came back from their much publicized jaunt somewhat disappointed. They were disillusioned with the guru because they said they had been looking for something special but had found him to be only human after all. A very enlightening statement!

Gurus became regular visitors on college campuses, and the youth of the West listened to their philosophies and found something in them that rang a bell. Book sales soared in unexpected areas. Youngsters began to plow through such treatises as *I Ching* (which Carl Jung swore by) and *The Practice of Detachment According to Zen. The Prophet* sold over three million copies, while *The Occult Dictionary for the Millions* became just that.

Late one night just as I returned to my home, I received an urgent phone call asking me to meet with someone who wanted to see me. I drove to the appointed place and waited for the person concerned, but I wasn't sure whom I was expecting, as I had never met him. Eventually he arrived with his girl friend. They were the epitome of the hippie culture in dress, attitude and experience. Their story was quite something. Both were excellent students in high school, both went to college and both dropped out in about ten weeks. They went to live in a commune and submerged themselves in the hippie scene, and had been there for about three or four years.

The boy came from a Jewish background and the girl from one of the more formal Christian denominations. Both had rejected the faith of their fathers and were sold on the mystical religions. The purpose of their visit with me was to show me where Christianity had failed and to present to me the advantages of Zen Buddhism. We had a great time together, and I enjoyed the time spent with these young people even though we didn't see eye-to-eye on anything very much.

Young people like this are not uncommon today. They have rebelled against a faith that is rational. They have no time for dogma, they resent restriction and they much prefer the experiential to the doctrinal. Their love affair with the Eastern religions came about like many love affairs. They were caught on the rebound after a disappointing experience. Both of the young people I have just mentioned had had some experience with religious teaching and spiritual exposure, but in both cases they had been confronted with religion without reality. And they had decided that that was not for them and so they had looked elsewhere. Thousands are in the same boat heading down the same river on voyages of discovery.

Not all the young people think like this. But those who don't are probably onto something not dissimilar —Astrology. "The Age of Aquarius" is not just a lively pulsating song from the musical, *Hair*. It is the theme tune of some lively pulsating kids who dig the stars and think that in some strange way their destiny is wrapped up in them. So they study the stars and their horoscopes diligently. They talk with great animation and enthusiasm about whether they are "Sagittarius," "Taurus" or "Cancer." They were very helpful to me and explained that I was "Scorpio" and my personality was characterized by power and determination and that I would make my mark on people and life. All very exciting!

Daily horoscopes provide a diet of instant advice and encouragement which the young avidly devour. They come as a substitute for a conscience, a guideline from the blue, and they give a sense of purpose to an otherwise meaningless existence. The stars don't make demands on people, which makes Astrology very popular. "It doesn't *compel,* it just *impels!*" said an expert. All that is necessary is to live in harmony with the stars in order that the persons concerned might fit into the pattern drawn in the stars at the moment of their birth. It is an interesting fact that astrologers tell people what they want to know. They find something flattering to say about everyone and keep all their customers in a good frame of mind. For instance, the same gentleman whose writings told me about my wonderful personality had something equally wonderful to say about all his customers. It didn't matter which of the twelve Zodiacal signs they were born under.

So great has been the demand for daily horoscopes that most daily newspapers carry them, the weeklies and monthlies carry them and even televised shows are avilable. Maurice Woodruff, known by some as the Brightest Star of Astrology has a newspaper column which has been syndicated around the world and has a combined circulation in excess of fifty million. He receives up to five thousand letters a week from people seeking his advice. Astrology is *big!*

Most young people in college have fooled around with ouija boards at light-hearted seances. Most get tired of it, some get frightened by it, but some are hooked by it. But a new thing has developed recently.

Bored by the innocuous times they were having with their ouija boards, the kids looked for something more exciting. And not a few of them came up with Satanism. This is not a light-hearted thing at all. This is for real.

A friend of mine, who has conducted many missions to students in different parts of the world, was holding a series of meetings in a well-known British university. He was used to opposition and was no stranger to ridicule, but at this particular time, he was aware of something new. One day he had occasion to visit a dormitory block in the university, and to his amazement he saw that every door had a sheep's skull nailed to it . . . a symbol of the devil worship in which the occupant of the room was involved. Immediately he knew the reason for the opposition and the strange forces which seemed to be at work in the university. He was up against people who had sold their souls to the devil and were actively engaging in Satan worship.

This kind of phenomenon has been on the increase in recent years, particularly among young people. The Church of Satan in San Francisco has a growing following of people who believe in black magic, curses and as much indulgence as possible.

The late Bishop Pike, with his remarkable knack of headline-hogging, captured the attention of the millions when he claimed to have had contact with his dead son. Tarot cards are in vogue, and everybody has some sneaky feeling about the mystical and Satanic undertones behind the Sharon Tate murder and the sordid saga of Charles Manson and his "family."

The mystical has superseded the rational; the experiential the doctrinal; the contemplative the active. But why? I believe that we have here another fascinating symptom of man's spiritual condition. He wants to understand the mysteries of the Universe. He longs to plumb the depths of his own person. Deep within him, he believes, lies the secret. Which secret, he knows not, but there must be one somewhere, somehow.

He longs for a feeling of security. Everything has to go right. The stars will tell him. Things must make sense, but he doesn't want to know the unpalatable— just the pleasant. The stars will give him that. He needs help with his decisions, and the certainty that his actions will be good, and the stars will tell him when to move and guarantee him success. He longs for meaning in life which the acquisition of material benefits has not given him. The "other world" must hold the clue to meaning. Tangible things don't have it. Intangibles must have it. Rationalism has led man into a maze of confusion. Mysticism must be where it's at. If I might just return to my two friends of whom I spoke earlier, I would like to tell you how excited I became as their search for meaning and security became more and more apparent to me. When I hear of the lengths to which the young people of our world are going in order to find answers that a vital experience of Christ can and does give, my convictions are confirmed.

CHAPTER 11

Meanwhile Back at the Church

Meanwhile, back at the church other problems exist. Doctrinal problems, personality problems, financial problems, denominational problems, "emphasis" problems, organizational problems! They are all very real and they are all very problematic, but are they all so serious that they should be allowed to take the time and interest and involvement of people from more pressing problems?

It is really a matter of objective. Does the church have an objective? If so, what is it? If not, why waste time on it? Many churches would be hard put to give a clear-cut statement of purpose that was more than a pious cliche inherited from earlier members. A "raison d'etre" is something that needs to be discovered and implemented quickly.

An old English preacher said that *the whole purpose of the whole church is to bring the whole Gospel to the whole world!* Now, there's a "raison d'etre!" It bears looking into. The *whole* purpose—not an incidental that can be fitted into the church's program where convenient. The *whole* Church, not just a lunatic fringe that is bent on pushing its ideas down unwilling throats. The *whole* Gospel—not just proof texts and easy steps to eternal bliss, but *all* the Gospel with its unapologetic demands and its unequivocal statements. The *whole* world—not just *us*. The favored few—the divine favorites. The *whole* world—that includes the mission fields from which the oceans protect us and the mission fields that swing and scream on our doorsteps.

This kind of objective makes some of our achievements and attitudes look green about the gills. This kind of vision helps put so many other things into focus. Doctrine is of prime importance, but ecclesiastical nit-picking is not. A world view helps us see this. The fact that Mrs. Smith threatened to leave the church because the pastor didn't shake her hand on Sunday is important to Mrs. Smith, but a wider view would help her considerably. Finances, unfortunately, are important, but not as important as we make them. So a view of what we are supposed to be doing will help us see that figuring out who is going to pay for the flowers on Sunday doesn't really matter so much. In fact, if we all got so busy doing what God gave us to do and hadn't the time or energy for the flowers, I'm sure that God would understand!

What color the men's room is painted is important to some and that's fine. Particularly if those to whom it is so important are going to show up on Saturday to slap the paint on the wall. But if the church started to do what she is supposed to be doing, the wall might even peel a little, and it wouldn't be the end of the world.

Majoring on minors is an easy thing to do, and the church is as guilty of this as anyone. Sometimes because the majors are embarrassing, sometimes because they are too challenging, but often because the people concerned haven't been told which is which. They wouldn't be able to tell a major from a minor if their life depended on it!

People are *major . . .* the *Gospel* is *major . . . getting the Gospel to the people* is *major . . . the untouched generation* is *major . . . the unreached scene* is *major . . . the rising generation that will soon account for half the Nation's population* is *major.*

As we have tried to show, the youth of today is searching. The immensity of their search and the urgency of their situation puts them near the top of my list of priorities for the church. But what on earth can the church do?

The first thing that the church can do is check on attitudes. There are a number to be seen in the pews. For instance, the good old time reactionary attitude! This attitude springs from a desire to preserve the old things. It produces Defenders of the Faith—and we need them. But it has its problems, for it falls into the trap of wanting to preserve things simply because they are old and distrusting new things just because they are *new*.

"As it was in the beginning, is now and ever shall be, world without end. Amen," is as good a description of this attitude as we need. It distrusts new translations of the Bible because they are new. It seems to have the mistaken idea that God wrote the King James Bible in olde tyme Englishe. It reacts against a new order of service. It has problems adjusting to new pastors. It feels that for music to be holy and sacred, it must have come from the pen of Wesley or Sankey. And quite understandably, it finds modern youth too much.

The "good old days" were undoubtedly good—but not all that good. For "distance lends enchantment to the view," and looking at those days from twenty, thirty, forty years' range allows you to forget the unpleasantness. But the reactionary-minded saints can't see that. They equate "old" with "good" and "new" with "bad," and it is hard for them to think otherwise. The good old days aren't here anymore, so they are not particularly relevant. What we did then is not necessarily going to be of any help in deciding what we are to do now. Kids as they were are not like kids as they are now. We've got to think again.

My first experience of the reactionary attitude of some of God's people took me completely by surprise. A group of us had contacted a number of young people whom we had been able to lead to Christ, and so the next thing was to take them to church. This we did and started a furor. The kids dressed in their normal clothes which could not be described as meeting the requirements of "Sunday best." But as they hadn't ever gone to church, we didn't see how they could suddenly be expected to produce the right uniform. It was an English service so there was some bobbing up and down. The kids occasionally bobbed up when they should have bobbed down, but they had never done this sort of thing before. So I did not think too much about it. To be truthful I only knew when to go up or down by keeping my eye on the old lady in front of me. The offering plate came by, and a stage whisper echoed along our row, "How much did you get?" And when the preacher asked a rhetorical question they answered it. No one had told them they weren't supposed to answer.

The deacons of that church called a hurried meeting, and I was deeply impressed by their alacrity, for by the time we had rounded up our herd and got them to the back door, the deacons had proposed, seconded, discussed and passed a resolution that we should be asked not to bring the young people back again—and this they duly did. We were "persona non grata." This was my first experience, but by no means the last.

Joses the Cypriot could have been a reactionary. He had his land and his religion, his traditions and his culture. But he was no reactionary, even when he had good cause to be.

Take the business of Saul of Tarsus, the rabble rouser. He disturbed meetings, blasphemed the name of Christ. He was violent, and the whole church must have had the heeby-jeebies whenever his name was mentioned. Then word got around that he had been converted. But everyone knew that old Ananias was naive and would believe anything. So the church gave this Saul the cold shoulder treatment, purely out of fear. They figured that it was his way of infiltrating their ranks. They didn't trust him, like him, want him or tolerate him. But, "Praise God," Cyprus Joe was different. (By this time they called him, Barnabas, incidentally.) He stuck his neck out, got hold of Saul, took him to church and asked for an interview with the board. He presented Saul to them, gave him a chance to testify, and Saul was accepted, but not too willingly.

Take the business of young John Mark. He had a chance to travel with Paul and Barnabas, became homesick, chickened out and fled the coop! Paul was furious, but Barnabas said, "Give him another chance." "Over my dead body," said Paul. They had a real argument about it, agreed to differ, and Paul took Silas, and Barnabas took Mark—and God made a man out of him. Barnabas is one of the first people I want to meet in heaven, because if he had reacted as did most of his contemporaries the church wouldn't have had Paul or Mark, and that would have left quite a hole in the New Testament.

This reactionary attitude lacks compassion, and that is obviously wrong. It isn't any good talking about the love of God from the pulpit if there is no love of God shown in concern and compassion from the pew. Some of the young people with whom I have talked are quite blunt when I ask them, "Do you ever go to church?" They reply, "Do you go where you're not wanted? Do you attend places where you are going to be insulted? Do you spend your time with people who despise you? Do you?"

As a result the reactionary lacks the ability to get close to and communicate with the young. This is a major tragedy. Because if the church doesn't communicate the truth to them, no one else will—and they will be fed on the diet of untruth that is so readily available to them.

An old missionary friend of mine asked me a good question one day. "Why did the church that started life as the most revolutionary event the world has ever seen degenerate into the most reactionary piece of the Establishment that the world has ever known?" That is a great thought, and it needs answering and confronting.

One reason, as I have already said, is fear. And fear is perfectly natural, which means that it isn't very spiritual! I think I understand the parents who want to keep their children away from any possible contamination, but I'm glad that God didn't adopt that attitude with His Son. I think I can understand the thinking of those who say that if you want to rear your kids to be Christians, you will have to protect them from every form of evil. A number of church people accordingly reserve the right to bar from their premises anyone who in their opinion would be detrimental to their own young people. But I don't agree with them for three reasons.

First, because it is anti-Biblical and anti-Spirit of Christ. Second, because you don't breed healthy kids by isolation, but by careful innoculation. Third, because you never fulfill your God-given responsibility to those "questionable" people.

As far as our children are concerned, my wife and I have given a great deal of serious thought to the problem. We don't feel that we love our children any less than do other parents, nor do we feel that we are careless in our spiritual concern for them. But we do feel that they should not be isolated from the world as it is, but rather given the chance through our ministry not only to see it as it is, but also to see that the Lord can do something about it through us. In this way they learn the problem and the answer and lose their fear in getting excited about a Lord who is bigger than all the problems they and their contemporaries are facing.

I am willing to be proved wrong about this, but I sincerely hope that I am not. Last week I asked my kids who are twelve, ten and eight, what they thought about the appearance of some of the youngsters with whom we have been working. "Weird," was their unanimous opinion.

When our daughter met a girl who had become pregnant out of wedlock, we told her what had happened, what the consequences would be and how the girl needed the Lord. She understood, not only the dilem-

71

ma of the girl but also our love for her and, most important, Christ's relevance to her. I think she now knows enough about this particular problem to be alert to it. But in addition she knows compassion for those who fall into the problem. And, most important, she knows how to share Christ where He is desperately needed.

I sympathize with the very real fears and tensions of many of the Lord's people. I have had them and do have them. But I never had a tension that the Holy Spirit couldn't conquer, and I have learned that the degree in which they conquer me is the degree in which He isn't allowed to conquer them!

CHAPTER 12

If You Can't Beat 'em, Join 'em

"If you want to talk about the church, forget it. But if you want to talk about Jesus Christ, I'll talk all night," a young man once said to me as our conversation took a spiritual turn.

"I would love to give my life to Christ, but does it mean that I would have to start attending church?" asked another youngster whom I was counseling.

"If Jesus Christ came back to earth and saw what you have done to His church, He would sue you," were the sentiments expressed by Cliff Richard in the Billy Graham movie, "Two A-Penny."

Many of the youth of today are anti-church. That does not mean they are disinterested in Christianity or antagonistic to the Gospel. Many of the young people whom I have contacted with the message of Christ actually have been very excited about Him and the truth—but they are anything but excited about the church.

Ignorance is one cause. They just don't know what is going on. In England one fellow was taken to church for the first time and was horrified to see the Vicar proceeding down the aisle resplendent in his cassock and surplice, swinging his incense. The boy leaped to his feet, spread out his arms and shouted, "Look out, Mrs., your handbag's on fire." The trappings of ecclesiastical tradition were definitely not for him.

Irrelevance is another cause, or what they take to be irrelevance. Many of the songs as well as the sermons and much of the language seem to be from another era. They are relics of a lost age. The prayers sound as if they are being addressed to an antiquated deity presiding over the dissolution of His once great Universe—and little, if anything, seems to be alive with the vitality of youth or fresh with the fresh-*ness* of a God who is way ahead of the times.

Impatience is another cause. The kids are impatient with anything that speaks of authority or moves with the slowness of a procedure that must go through the correct channels! "Why do they have to look like that and sing like that and pray like that and organize like that and dress like that and just be like that?" "We don't want to take on their mantle. We don't want to be pressed into their mold or modeled after their pattern. We are a different breed of cat."

It's this kind of talk that has added fuel to the flame of fear in many of the older people in the church. "Who do they think they are, coming in here and disrupting our worship, dressing like that and behaving like that? We are not going to tolerate it, or them. If they want to be like that, they can start their own church—*and pay for it*. But while *we* are paying for this one, it will be done *our* way."

I can understand this feeling, and I have a certain amount of sympathy for this attitude. However, there are some older people, while they have the interests of the young at heart, who are unwittingly making a serious mistake in this area. They are the exact opposites of the reactionaries of whom we spoke earlier, the believers in the "We've always done it this way" philosophy. They are as revolutionary as the others are reactionary. "If you can't beat 'em, join 'em," is their approach.

The mere hint of tradition infuriates them. They reject ideas merely because they have a tinge of history. Overboard with the whole works and on board with anything that is new! New things are tried for no other reason but that they are new. Old things are discarded for no other reason but that they are old. "If it's old, it must be bad, and if it's new, it's just got to be good."

"If we don't do it the way the kids demand it, we'll never get to them," they preach.

They really want the church to become a puppet manipulated by the young, dancing to any tune the kids want to whistle. And this is their error. I am not sure in my own mind which is worse—the reactionary attitude that rejects the kids out of hand or the revolutionary attitude that does everything their way. Neither will get very far.

There are some folks who tell me that if you are going to communicate with the young, you must dress like them. I don't know of anything quite so out of place as a pastor trying to look like a youthful hippie. His every move shrieks, "Phony!" He is trying to masquerade as something he obviously isn't and be something he couldn't be even if he could turn the clock back fifteen years. The kids don't need any help in spotting phonies. They can see them a mile off. Some of the most effective people in the area of contemporary youth work are people in their middle years who look as if they are in their middle years and thereby bring the stability of those years to the youth who are living in turmoil. It is their obvious stability that is so attractive.

One well-dressed mother asked me about a lady who led a Bible study which her son attended. "Tell me about this woman," she said, her voice sharp with hostility. "She must be a real swinger to attract boys my son's age." With great amusement I proceeded to disillusion her by describing a lady past fifty. I told the mother to ask her son what the Bible teacher was like, and the next time I saw her she gave me his answer. "Motherly," he had told her. "She just loves us." The mother had flashed back, "Are you suggesting that I don't love you?" "No," he replied, "I'm not suggesting that at all, but you don't love me in the way she can because she has God's love in her." The ones who say everything must be done to cater to the young people are in my opinion sadly mistaken. It isn't the way you look that matters in the long run. It's the way you love them through thick and thin that counts.

Then there is the thorny matter of music. "If we are going to get the kids, we'll have to have their kind of music." Some churches have given their organists the golden handshake and installed drums and guitars and various other instruments of music and torture. Amplified to the limits of audio-endurance, their music has shattered the eardrums, the nerves and the tempers of everyone over thirty. All idea of worship has disappeared. "In quietness and confidence shall be your strength," has gone down the drain, and any concept of dignity in the presence of God has disappeared.

I am not suggesting that it takes drums and guitars to do this. I've had many organists blast my message through the stained glass windows with some fugue or other that was not designed to bring the message home to people's hearts, but rather to show how good the organist is at his profession.

"Getting high on Jesus," 'Turned on to Christ," "The Jesus Freaks" are terms that have become currently in vogue. I am less than enthusiastic about their usage, because I have no time for the drug scene at all, and I want none of its connotations carried over into an experience of Christ. I have no objection to the use of valid means of communication, but I believe that the "means" of communication should be compatible with the "matter" being communicated. So when a kid is allowed or even encouraged to bring the hip language of an experience diametrically opposed to Christ into his new experience of Christ, I believe that his advisers are doing him a grave disservice. Not only are they doing him an injustice but the church as well. Can anyone tell me the spiritual value of the following "testimony" to an assembly of people, "When I turned on to Jesus, it was like 'Wow,' Man. Ya gotta get with it, Man. Jesus is where it's at, Man. It's like 'Wow,' Man, 'Wow'."

To the people over thirty the young lady was communicating nothing but her lack of grammar and the poverty of her vocabulary. To the younger folks she was talking their language but saying little. And that is one of the main problems of the revolutionary approach. It lacks depth—depth of understanding. Any Christian experience that is allowed to stay in the shallows will eventually evaporate like the shallows. And any Christian leadership that majors on the "If you can't beat 'em, join 'em" approach may have instant apparent success, but it will run the risk of disappearing as quickly as it appeared.

It has been my unhappy lot to visit groups of young people whose misguided leaders have joined the kids in their ignorance instead of leading them into greater depths. They are pitiful groups because they know nothing of anything except elementals. They live in the realm of the experiential, which in their case is limited, and spend much of their time sharing very little and pooling their ignorance. Those youngsters have a greater potential than they are being encouraged to discover. They could enjoy deeper experiences of Christ than they will ever enjoy unless and until someone leads them to a higher level of which they are totally ignorant.

Another problem is that this kind of approach produces kids who lack discipline. I am fully aware that discipline is a dirty word, but I am equally aware that discipline and discipleship are close relatives. And Jesus didn't commission the church to produce anything but disciples. Any youth outreach that does not have as its objective the production of well-trained, deeply-taught, thoroughly motivated disciples is missing the boat. And I have yet to be convinced that this can be done by joining the kids in their ill-disciplined condition, pampering them in their caprices and discarding those things that the kids find hard to stomach for no other reason than that they don't like them.

God's kind of Christianity is a warfare and a spiritual revolution. It always has been, and it always will be. The men in the vanguard of its growth and in the forefront of its conflict have been men who gladly learned to live with the things they didn't like, they learned to swallow the distasteful and they had backbone in their wishbone. They learned not by instinct and not by applying a Christian veneer to their non-Christian life, but by their willingness to expose themselves to the teachings of leaders who demanded in Christ's name totally different attitudes and behavior.

Which brings us to another problem area. Kids who are lacking in spiritual depth and discipline always lack distinction. They are no different than their contemporaries. Or if they are, but don't appear so, they have a hard time persuading anyone to believe them. The difference should be so obvious that people are moved to inquire about it. A boy whom I led to Christ in Wales told me about his experience.

One day a teacher in his school stopped him in the corridor and said, "What happened to you, David?" David immediately tried to think of what he had done wrong, but he couldn't, so he played for time and said, "Nothing, sir, nothing happened to me." "Don't say that nothing has happened to you when I can see something has happened to you. Your work is different. Your attitude is different. Your behavior is different. *You're* different," the teacher insisted. Then it dawned on David, and he said, "Oh, yes, sir, I was converted."

The teacher snorted, turned on his heel and walked away and thereby showed himself to be a fool. For he had seen a difference, inquired about what he had seen, asked for and received an explanation, and rejected it because it clashed with his preconceived ideas. But David had made his point. Distinction is imperative.

It may sound as if I insist that all young people who come to Christ get their hair cut immediately, squeeze themselves into collars and ties and buy themselves a Sunday suit. Not at all! I would no more try to legislate external lengths of hair or skirt as a barometer of spiritual caliber than I would use church attendance as a guarantee of spiritual maturity. But I would expect to see some changes, perhaps over a period of weeks, or sometimes months, and I might even have to settle for years.

I want my attitude toward young people to be one that shows I am sympathetic to them, but not subservient to them. I want to be different but not dyed-in-the-wool. I would say quite honestly that it is relatively simple to react against them totally or to join forces with them completely. The difficult route is to maintain the right kind of distance that produces the respect without which leadership does not exist and to have the kind of contact that keeps the lines of communication open—to get the balance between being so "with it" that you have their ear—and being so different that they know where they are going in their new life with Christ.

CHAPTER 13

Love 'em or Lose 'em

Recently our church experienced something of a youthful invasion. We already had a fair-sized group of young people who were the children of church members, but these new kids were something else—in more ways than one! Naturally their arrival caused quite a stir. Some were delighted to see them, others were anything but delighted. But there they were.

My feelings were somewhat ambivalent. I have worked with young people for many years and accordingly have a real love for them. But I was pastor of a church that has a ministry for all ages, and therefore I had a responsibility to the older people as well.

Of one thing I had no doubts and this was that there is a place in the church of Jesus Christ for *all* people. The Lord said that the hallmark of His people which would show they were His disciples was *love*. Now, if love in the church is to show itself to the world in such a way that it is unique, it has to be something absolutely "out of this world." What is so "out of this world" about a group of middle-class, middle-aged Republicans getting along together? What is so "out of this world" about blacks keeping to themselves or kids keeping away from deacons? Is that what He was talking about? Is it that kind of love which was going to be so special? Of course not.

The kind of love that makes the world sit up and take notice is the kind that cuts across all known barriers—and that is what the church has to portray. A barrier-crossing, prejudice-banishing love! What an opportunity these kids were handing us on a platter—to show the kind of love to them that would in turn make the world say, "Hey, did you hear about what happened in that church?"

So I knew that the oldsters and the youngsters had to be molded together in the Lord. And not only because of the love demonstration. The pattern of the early church is something to which we must continually refer. There they had a happy blend of youth and age. Paul the aged and Timothy the youngster got along fine. John the youth and Peter the older man were firm friends as well as brothers. There was room for Philemon and Onesimus, Barnabas and John Mark— and they were all made to feel they had a place. Paul told Timothy, "Don't let them look down their noses at you because you are young, and don't think you can run the show either, because you must recognize and respect an elder."

So I had no problem knowing what I was supposed to do, but I wasn't too sure about how to do it. I asked my older people to be patient. I shared with them my concern for the young people. I preached the wonder-working power of the Risen Lord who could choose Simon the Zealot and Matthew the Publican in His Twelve and bind them together. Simon and the others have been on my mind so much recently! When the Romans invaded Palestine, Simon went underground and became a revolutionary, while Matthew stayed above ground and became a collaborator. I told my people, "If Jesus the Lord can handle that one, our problem is chicken feed." Most of them came along. Some hung back with a "wait-and-see" attitude. Others left.

Then I went to the kids. I told them, "You are as welcome in the church as anyone and everyone. You come as often as you wish, and you will have a real heartfelt welcome from me. I want you here. But this attitude is not shared by all the people, and I know why. They are afraid of you. And looking at you I can understand that, too. Because you do look weird.

Now I want you to do comething for me. Help me sell you to the older folks. I'm going to bat for you, and I need your support. Don't do anything that will give your critics any grounds for criticism. Be alert to them. They are watching and waiting for you to step out of line. Remember this!"

I went on, "These people are great people who love the Lord so much that they have built up a church, provided the ministry you want, built facilities you have chosen to use, and generally made available to you many things that you could not make available to yourselves. Therefore, respect them and thank them and show your appreciation by listening to what they say. Try to please them and demonstrate love to them. Don't gripe about them not loving you if you aren't loving them."

The kids listened and responded. They accepted the exhortation because they felt it was reasonable. *And that is the key!* If they feel you are for real, have their interests at heart and have something exciting to offer them, they will be some of your most enthusiastic supporters and workers. Then I talked to them about specifics, like appearance and behavior. I asked them to try to be tidy and aware of the feelings of others. "But I don't have a suit, I've only got jeans," shouted one boy. "You weren't listening," I replied. "I didn't mention a suit, I said 'tidy' so if in your opinion you can be tidy in jeans and you feel that you can wear jeans to church after you have carefully considered the feelings of others, then in jeans you must come."

It has been interesting to see how they have come. Most of them, tidily, most of them contemporarily, but none of them could be mistaken for members of the older generation by the wildest stretch of the imagination! Right now, I am satisfied with the progress on both sides of the fence! Both groups have made a real effort, and they have all had refreshing encounters and valuable experiences learning from each other.

It is imperative that the church should steer a clear course between the two ditches that could swallow any ministry that she must have to the rising generation. These are the ditch of "overreaction" and the ditch of "overindulgence." One communicates nothing, and the other is more interested in the business of communicating than the contents communicated. Call it "middle-of-the-road" if you will. I prefer to call it—*balance*.

Paul said, "Let your moderation be known to all men." And that doesn't mean be moderately good or moderately bad. Or be moderately enthusiastic or moderately lazy. Nor does it mean moderately short shorts or moderately long dresses. Or moderate amounts of makeup or money. Neither is moderation mediocrity. Moderation means "sweet reasonableness." That's what the youth situation needs. Sweet reasonableness from old to young and back again!

To get it you need a clear understanding of what is going on. That takes time and effort and much eating of words and swallowing of pride. It requires a listening ear and a beating heart. Then it takes a sympathetic attitude. This isn't hard to come by if you stop poking at what people do and try to find out why they do it.

Just a few days ago a veteran Christian worker known to thousands told me in tears that young people irritate him beyond endurance. He said, "They hate me, and it's because I hate them so much. They despise me because I have no interest in them and have no time for them. I say one thing from the pulpit and practice another where they are concerned." I encouraged him to try and see *why* they did what they did and not to allow *what* they did to stick in his gullet. He started humbly to ask them things. He inquired about them, talked with them, opened his heart to them, told them he didn't understand them, explained that he wanted to get to them and asked them to help him.

They responded to him. The following day he stood and testified to the miracle the Lord had worked in his heart because he had been willing to learn why they ticked as well as seeing a lot of ticks he didn't like. Then smiling through his tears, he said to a group of ministers, "When I had finished talking with the young people, one young man said it was a privilege to work with me. No one had told me that in forty years. Then a young lady came and kissed me." He blinked shyly and added, "No one had done that in forty years either!"

Some years ago I was leading an outreach in an industrial town in England. We needed much help from the Christian constituency. This wasn't coming as we had hoped. One afternoon I was asked to eat with some of the Christian leadership of the city, and as soon as I sat down the hostess said, "Stuart Briscoe, I hate you." Did you ever start a social engagement on that happy note?

"Oh, how interesting," I replied, being a typical Englishman, somewhat taken aback!

"You embarrassed me into having to go to some of those dreadful young people that you were working among," she went on. "I didn't want to go, but I knew I had to go because of my position in the Christian work of this city. And I blamed you for the embarrassment because if you hadn't suggested such a crazy outreach I would not have been put in this position. However, I went down to the place and decided I would look in and get out before I was contaminated. At least then I would have been able to say that I had been there."

She continued, "When I saw those young people, all my worst fears were confirmed, and I turned to leave when a complete stranger came up to me and asked if I was a Christian. When I answered in the affirmative, the stranger led me to a scruffy little girl and told me to lead her to Christ. I looked at her and took an instant dislike to her but couldn't get out of the fix I was in. So I started to talk with her, and her story broke my heart. She had never had a chance. She needed the Lord, and I led her to Christ. And that kid got to me. I want you to know that I still hate what you did to put us all in that position, but I can't thank you enough." I breathed again! Then one after another the dinner guests said basically the same things, and I realized that the Christian leadership of that city—busy in their work in Christ's name—had never taken the time to try to understand that under every skin there lies a story, and often the shaggier the skin, the sadder the story.

There are no substitutes for understanding and sympathy. And there is a tremendous need for conviction. Conviction that the Gospel is relevant to the youth of today! I know every Christian would say that the Gospel is relevant if asked, but I don't think that every Christian really believes it.

"Beyond redemption," you will hear them say of some.

"They are hopeless."

"Turn the National Guard on them."

These and other such charming statements are sentiments I have heard from the lips of some of God's frozen people. But a real heart-burning conviction that the Gospel is the thing that can turn the tide in the youth situation is what I mean by conviction.

Is the drug explosion symptomatic of a search for expansion of the consciousness?

Then Christ offers that.

Is the sex explosion a search for love and satisfaction?

Then Christ gives that.

Is the pop explosion a search for ideas and communication of those ideas?

Then Christ can cope with some real ideas.

Is the fashion explosion a search for identity?

Then Christ answers that one.

Is the revolution, protest, explosion a search for liberty and a cause?

Christ gives both in superlative measure.

Is mysticism a search for reality?

Christ said, "I am the Truth" and truth is reality.

Is communal living a search for brotherhood?

The family of Christ is the greatest commune there ever was or will be.

When a person really believes he has the message that alone answers the needs of the youth of today, he is a man of conviction. Add conviction to understanding, mix it with a dash of sympathy and pour it out in the direction of the youth of today, and the mixture will produce the desired effects. It will also keep those who long to reach the kids from excesses on either hand. And this is so important.

Many people have asked me, "But when you are in doubt about certain things, where do you draw the line?" This is not easy to answer, but my own approach is basically simple. First, I ask myself, "Do the Scriptures say anything specific on this point?" If they do, then I must act accordingly. If they do not, I ask myself, "Do the Scriptures lay down any principles that I can apply to this issue?" Often I find that they do. This is where many of our answers are to be found . . . not always in black and white formal instructions like, "Do this, then do this and never do this," but more in terms of basic principles that we must apply to the modern situation.

If I still can't come up with any clear guidance I apply the motto, "When in doubt, cool it." This I have found necessary over and over again. So often the things we can irritate by our intrusion or legalism will be resolved quite simply by the application of love and patience.

For instance, a young man was asked to give a testimony to a group of ladies to whom my wife was speaking. She was asked to take the boy (a new Christian) with her. His hair was quite long, and she wondered what she should do about it. Should she quote First Corinthians 11:14 and hope that he wouldn't ask, "How long is long?" Or perhaps point out to him that Absalom's long hair was a matter of considerable admiration in his day, but long hair was a "shame" in Greece in Paul's day, and that therefore it was obvious that styles changed with the years and attitudes with geographical locations.

On the other hand she had a feeling that the ladies to whom he was to speak might take offense at his appearance and not hear his words. But she need not have worried for the boy arrived with his hair cut—not very short, but shorter than it had been in years. She asked him why he had done it, and he said, "Because speaking for the Lord is so important to me that I didn't want anything to get in the way."

The ladies were told this and then were asked, "How would you feel if your appearance was a hindrance to the Gospel? Would you change your life style? Not because you felt it wrong, but simply because you thought more about the people to whom you were speaking than your own feelings about your appearance?"

That boy shook that meeting apart. If he had been told to cut his hair, he probably would have objected or done it reluctantly. But he wasn't, and the Lord won a victory through him that day. Incidentally I noticed on Sunday that his locks are lengthening again. Maybe he needs another preaching engagement!

What a relief it is to know that in all these things God has promised to all who lack wisdom the wisdom they need. I draw on that promise all the time. I need continual wisdom to stay realistic and avoid being reactionary or revolutionary.

CHAPTER 14

The "Push-Off-the-Deep-End" Policy

But what about the kids who have been raised in the church and have never been on drugs or engaged in all the other vices we have been discussing? They certainly must not be ignored, and sometimes I think there is the danger that they may be. There is no doubt that there are many fine youngsters in this category who are a credit to their homes and their churches. Thousands of them have made their mark over the years, but I feel that a word of caution is not out of place.

As a Britisher I feel there are not many things that the church in England can teach the church in America, but there are some. Perhaps the main one is how to recognize the trends. You see, England may not lead America in many things, but she is way ahead in apostasy. In England it is no longer the fashionable thing to go to church. It hasn't been since the War. The vast majority of families never attend church, and a large percentage of the rest only go at the "recognized times." This has had a remarkable effect on the youth of the land. I have worked in towns where over ninety-five percent of the youth never attended church.

Now here is the word of warning. I detect signs of boredom among many of the American church's young people that frighten me. They are turning off the things of God and are simply going to church because they are expected to, or told to—or both, but there is no interest whatsoever.

At the present rate of regress I would say that America could be level with England in less than two generations. Apostasy could be just around the corner. A Sunday school teacher of many years' experience told me recently that when he asked his kids what they would like to study and discuss in Sunday school, he was told, "It doesn't make any difference to us. We are not interested and we don't believe any of it. We are only here because we are made to come, but as soon as we are old enough to please ourselves, we won't be here. So do what you like—we could care less." Thoroughly disinterested and bored, these kids are going to be an ever-increasing problem.

For some time I used to think that the youth of to-day posed two problems to the church. *Problem No. 1:* The unreached kids outside! *Problem No. 2:* The bored kids inside! I have had more experience with Problem No. 1 and accordingly find Problem No. 2 harder to take. Unreached kids are ignorant of the truth, but when they are approached correctly they can quickly become interested. Bored kids have had just enough truth to be inoculated against it and thus are very difficult to handle.

But let us return to the two problems. I found out that there aren't really two problems—there is only one. They are two halves of the big one. The un-reached kids are unreached because the bored kids are bored. If that is true, then the answer to both is in the singular. There is but one answer. Set the "bored" kids to reach the "unreached" and by doing that, not only will the "unreached" be reached, but the "bored" kids will have no time to be bored. How about that for killing two birds with one stone?

In my opinion this has to be a fundamental concept of modern church youth work. I feel that many churches at their present rate of progress will never reach the mass of modern kids. Given two or three millennia, they would still not make it. Also at the rate things are moving among their "own" kids, they won't have them much longer, either. Soon they must begin to accept the validity of this idea. Then they must do something about it.

Most church youth programs I have seen in America are geared more to the preservation of the redeemed than the evangelization of the lost. Therefore, I feel that a basic change of gears is necessary. Programs should be introduced that will get the church kids mobilized to reach the unreached. *Mobilization* is a big word here.

In my experience, when a church gets around to thinking about mobilization to reach the youth of today, they think of the Youth Pastor arranging some more meetings. That may be fine, but it is not what I am talking about. I'm not interested in getting the Youth Pastor to do more, while his kids watch him perform with varying degrees of interest or disinterest. I am thinking in terms of getting the church kids to do the work. Getting other people to perform a task (particularly young people) is often harder than doing it yourself, and therefore many leaders take the relatively easy course and do it all, while the rest of the folks let them. The leaders grumble about no one being interested, and the watchers grumble about leaders who want to run the whole show!

There is something else closely involved in mobilization—*motivation*. Right or wrong I once thought you have to get people rightly motivated before you can get them thoroughly mobilized. In many cases that could be true, but it is by no means the general rule.

When I joined the Marines, I was mobilized, but there was no motivation. It took time for me to become motivated to being a Marine and being proud of being a Marine. Then it took even more time for me to want to be an enthusiastic Marine. Maybe this is where we make some of our mistakes with the young people. We give long talks on motivation, preach sermons on responsibility and try to instill a sense of duty, but nothing much happens.

When I started preaching at seventeen years of age, I was mobilized, but not motivated. They came to me at my church and said, "Don't you think it's time you spoke at the youth meeting?"

"No, I don't think so. I can't preach," I replied.

"Have you ever tried?" was the next question.

"Er . . . no."

"Then how do you know you can't?"

I admitted that was a good point for which I had no answer and was told, "Okay, you preach on 'The Church at Ephesus' a week from Tuesday." I didn't even know they had a church at Ephesus, but suddenly I had a consuming passion to know all there was to know on the subject. Some wise character got me mobilized knowing that if he waited for me to get motivated, he might still be waiting when the Lord returned. But he achieved both. He succeeded in *motivating* and *mobilizing* me.

For the sake of brevity I call this approach, "the push-off-the-deep-end policy." Sometimes it is a disaster, but usually it works. The whole thing is basically simple. Give someone something to do, knowing that there are only two possibilities—they will either sink or swim. If they sink, pull them out, pump them out and then set them down and say, "You sank!" Ruefully, they will agree.

"Okay! Let's find out why you sank."

"You mean you're not mad at me?"

"Of course not. Why do you think you sank?"

I would say that on this approach you will very quickly build up a close rapport with the sinker and in no time turn him into a swimmer. When you see him swimming strongly, you'll get such a kick out of him because you know that if he hadn't been shoved in, he would still be dipping his toe in the shallow end. That's where many of our kids are. And that is where they stay—until you push 'em in.

On the other hand, of course, he might swim. I did

when I was pushed off the deep end of the pulpit. In fact, I swam so strongly I forgot about the time, and it wasn't until I noticed uneasiness among my contemporaries who were listening that I stole a surreptitious glance at the clock and saw I was overtime. Worse still—I had only finished one of my three points! That posed a different problem. They had to tell me how to stop. "Shut up and sit down," were the words, if I remember correctly. They then encouraged me by giving me another chance to finish my talk. Then they asked me to give another, and I'm still at it more than twenty years later. (Not the same talk!)

Of course, "pushing off the deep end" produces other problems, too. Like parents! Quite naturally, parents get a little perturbed if their kids come home and say, "Guess what we're going to do at church on Friday night?"

"Roller skating?"

"No."

"Swimming?"

"Try again."

"Barbecue?"

"Keep trying."

"Bowling?"

"Nope!"

"We're all going to be pushed off the deep end."

"The deep end? The deep end of what?"

"We're going to go on an outreach to the kids down at the drug store."

What's the pastor's telephone number?"

"Oh, mom, come on. Everybody's going."

"Is this the pastor? What's all this about my Agatha . . ." This is something that must be expected, and for which there is no easy answer, although I have sometimes suggested that the parent concerned might like to come along with us to the drug store. If they do, that's fine. If they don't, it usually gets them off the phone!

Naturally, the kids will be apprehensive, too. Some years ago in England I was leading a Bible school in which we had students from around the world. They sat dutifully at their desks listening to hours of lectures, copying yards of notes, and amassing tons of material. But I was uneasy about how much they were actually learning. So I approached some pastor friends and arranged for them to accommodate the students for a week in exchange for which the students would work in the church. I asked the pastors if they had any jobs that needed doing, particularly the kind of jobs that their people would not or did not do, and they said, "Lots!" It was agreed that the students should be given those jobs.

When I announced the plans to the students, an interesting development occurred. We had an epidemic of assorted illnesses. Everybody became sick. One fine big fellow came to me and said in a whisper, "I can't go."

"Why?"

"I've lost my voice."

"So, why can't you go?"

"I can't communicate."

"You could write it down, couldn't you?"

"Oh!"

Then on a hunch I said to him, "You really haven't lost your voice."

"I have," he insisted hoarsely.

"You haven't, you're just chicken."

He protested as violently as one can without a voice. Then I added, "Don't worry. Everyone is chicken. I am." He looked at me with amazement and *shouted,* "You're not." His voice "returned" immediately, and he had no more trouble with it. But his condition was common. We were all apprehensive, but someone was needed to be the first one to admit it. Then everyone was in it together. What a thrill to see those young people dive into the opportunity to do things they had

93

never done before. Practically everyone had stories to tell of their first attempts at swimming when they suddenly found themselves in the water.

One short, stocky Yorkshireman told about knocking on a door. It opened and there stood the biggest black man he had ever seen in his life. He towered over the student and roared, "Wha' d'ya wan'?" Believing that since he was already in the water there was no point wasting time, he answered bluntly, "To tell you about Jesus."

"Don' mention that name heah," yelled the man.

"Jesus," said the student.

"I said, 'Don' you say that word heah.' Ya heah me?"

"Jesus," he repeated.

"If ya say that again, I'll knock yore haid off yore shoulders."

"Jesus," he said, very softly, waiting for his head to leave his shoulders. It didn't, but in a very different tone of voice the man said, "All right, come in." He did go in and returned every day. Not only was the man he visited changed but the boy himself never recovered from the exciting experience of really feeling that God had proved Himself to him for the first time in his spiritual experience.

The ones who can be used chiefly in the great outreach to modern young people are the church young people. They will never do it while their leaders talk about it and their parents fret about it and their preachers preach about it. They will start when they get a good old push into the deep end.

CHAPTER 15

How Many "Trumps"?

If you want to bore your kids in church, give them a series of lectures entitled, "Why I believe in the existence of God." Go into all the arguments neatly labeled under the following headings:

1. The Ontological Argument.
2. The Teleological Argument.
3. The Cosmological Argument.
4. The Anthropological Argument.

That will really set 'em alight!

Let me show you a more effective way. Take the kids down to a place where there are some of the "other kind" of young people and tell them to talk about God to them. They might even try quoting John 3:16. But they will in all probability run into heavy weather, like this—

"For God . . ."

"Hold it. How do you know there's a God?"

"I've always believed it."

"Very impressive! Go on! What were you saying?"

". . . so loved the world . . ."

"Wait a minute. If He did, why did He let it get in this mess?"

"Humph! I don't really know, but I remember my Sunday school teacher saying something about . . ."

"Forget it."

That young Christian would come back rather deflated. You would need to sit down with him, encourage him and say to him, "Do you remember the arguments for the existence of God?" He probably wouldn't remember one of them, but I would guarantee that he would give anything to know. *Then*, you can start training him. He would be eager to learn as he had never been before.

Occasionally I have visited churches where the young people have become enthralled about reaching the unreached. So their leaders started a preparation program which went on and on and on—in fact, some of these programs have gone on so long preparing the young people that eventually no one can even remember what they were being prepared to do—and the young people have graduated to the Young Marrieds! Perhaps I have a nasty, suspicious mind, but I have suspected sometimes that the leaders of the young people are less than enthusiastic about the whole thing, and yet they can't say, "No," to their kids. But they dare not say, "Yes." So they compromise and say, "Let's prepare."

Now don't jump down my throat and say I am against adequate preparation, because I am not. I'm trying to show that the only way to motivate people to want preparation for this kind of activity is to give them a taste of it first. Then they will not need motivating to get prepared. They'll pull you to bits to get all the help they can.

Some years ago in Ireland my wife and I had a conference for young people. They came for the usual "fun and fellowship" but weren't particularly excited about the spiritual side of the conference. We shared with them some of our convictions, and they told us about the "get-together" they had every Sunday after church.

"What's it like?" we asked.

"A drag."

"What do you do?"

"Sing the same songs, hear the same words, then go home."

"Why do you go?"

The girls said, "To see the boys."

The boys said, "To see the girls."

"Why don't you go out on the streets and invite other kids to come in for a cup of coffee and tell them about the Lord?"

"Never thought of it. They wouldn't come. What would the leaders say?"

They tried it. The place was flooded with seekers. The kids got on the job and shared what they knew, which they soon discovered wasn't very much. Then they were eager to learn, and the right kind of people were reached.

But we had a problem. The leaders called me in and said, "We know that the young people are very happy about doing something, and we know that many young people are being reached. But we . . . er . . . feel . . . er . . . that it ought to stop."

"Really," I replied. "Why?"

"Too many Catholics are coming in!"

It is always a thorny problem when unenthusiastic young people in a church become enthusiastic, because they sometimes get the bit between their teeth and take off. The leaders who have spent years trying to achieve this without particular success, then find themselves trying to keep up with them. They spend their time picking up the bits, and this can be painful. Too many have decided it just isn't worth it, and they have squelched the whole thing, thereby doing inestimable harm to the kids.

Surely one thing that the church has failed to do is to realize the potential of youth. There are vast amounts of latent enthusiasm and talent lying dormant in churches around the world. Kids are natural enthusiasts. That means that any church that does not have enthusiastic young people in it has managed to rob their youth of one of their most precious inbuilt assets—and to rob a kid of enthusiasm you have to be a genius!

Kids are natural activists. They want to be doing.

In fact, I believe that young people thrive on *activity* and *adventure*. Furthermore, I believe that most youth programs deny them both. This would be bad enough if it wasn't so contrary to Biblical Christianity. Read the Acts of the Apostles and write across it *Activity* and *Adventure*. Then go to your kids who thrive on these two things, and if these are not apparent in their Christian experience, ask yourself some rather straight questions, like—"How on earth did I manage to rob them of a basic part of their makeup and deny them the stuff of which Christianity is made?" Good question!

Kids are naturally daring. The older you get, the wiser you get, I know. But you also get a lot more prosaic and predictable. You lose a lot of sparkle and zest and all the fundamentals that go to make excitement a part of your everyday life. You become like the old man who said, "My get-up-and-go has got up and went."

The natural daring of youth was brought home to me when I was in the Marine Commandos. We had a construction called the "Death Slide." It was a rope stretched from the top of a cliff to the bottom of a quarry at an angle of 45°. The Death Slide was used as a means of hasty exit from inhospitable territory. Therefore, all Commandos had to know how to throw a rope over it, hang on and leap into the void and slide furiously down. Halfway down, it was necessary to start running in mid-air so when you hit the ground, you hit it running. If you didn't, you hit the ground, period. And the next guy who couldn't stop in mid-air would hit you—and so on!

Would you believe that the Death Slide held many terrors for new recruits? We battled with them for days trying all we knew to get them to slide down the rope. Some we had to push off the cliff and listen to their screams fading in the distance. But we had a problem. Every night we had to dismantle the Death Slide because the kids of the nearby village were playing on it! The kids of the village *played* on what the Commandos were afraid to do.

We must recognize the precious potential of Christian youth, because it is a divine gift to the church which must not be allowed to become buried. In our youth lie the main reserves of energy and enthusiasm and daring, and any church that is not capitalizing on these reserves will have a ministry deficient in these critical areas.

When I was very young, I remember an old man giving a talk on the "Last Trump," that will sound at the return of Christ for His people. The old man made great emphasis on the fact that it was the *last* trump[et]. "Young people," he said, "it's the last trump, so don't try to go before the last trump." Immediately in my innocence I wondered how many "trumps" there would be, for I figured that if I didn't know how many there would be, I wouldn't know which was the last. So I asked the old man at the end of his talk. "How many trumps will there be?" His retort floored me, "Don't be impudent."

That incident has remained with me for a long time. He was talking nonsense, of course, and like a lot of people talking nonsense, he was very defensive about it. So when I asked a perfectly legitimate question on the basis of his exposition he became upset. Of course, this is an extreme case, but his kind are all too common.

"Don't ask questions. Just sit and listen."

"Don't query dogmatic facts. Swallow the dogma."

"Don't expect to do anything. Be quiet and concentrate on growing up."

Do you think that God intends for young people to sit in rows like cabbages and just listen to all they are being told? I don't think they are intended to be inactive until they are elected deacons. Do you think they should be expected to remain passive in church when every other part of their world encourages them to be active? I think that when God put youngsters in our churches, He gave us something He couldn't give us any other way.

"But they are so irresponsible," is the plaintive cry. Of course, they are irresponsible, because responsibility has to be learned, and there is only one way it can be learned . . . by being given responsibility. Many pastors that I know insist that a young person proves himself responsible, before he can ever be given any responsibility. I flatly disagree.

There was one boy in our youth club in England who was the "Champion Window Breaker." When he joined the club everyone said, "Watch your windows." But we didn't worry. We simply made him responsible for all the windows being kept intact and he never broke another. He was also an expert at seeing that no one else did either!

Of course you can give a young person responsibility and not let him function. Some people tell a youngster to do something and then spend every minute breathing down his neck to see if he's doing it. Or telling him, "That is not the way to do it." When we were kids we were like that. We would plant seeds and give them the responsibility of growing into plants, and then we would dig them up every few minutes to see how they were doing. Give him responsibility, tell him clearly what you want him to do and then leave him to it. But you must remember that if you have delegated a job to him you are still ultimately responsible, so when something goes wrong, don't say, "You idiot, why did you do that?" Because you are probably the reason he did "that." By failing to instruct him clearly or by not being approachable when he had a question, or perhaps because what you called "delegation" ought more correctly to be called "abrogation." Give him the chance to see if he can do it. Don't breathe down his neck as he's doing it. Be available to him while he's doing it. When he goes wrong, don't bawl him out. Stick with him. Show him where he went wrong and remember that "he who never made a mistake never made anything."

Kids are full of ideas. Crazy, zany, impractical, unsophisticated, wild, funny, challenging, frightening ideas are there just below their youthful skins. But you would never know it in many churches. "Now this is what we're going to do, kids. . . ." Instead of, "Hey, kids, what do you think we should do about so and so?" A loud silence will probably ensue if you try that approach. So you might be tempted to say, "I knew it. Not a sensible idea in their heads." But you would be wrong. There are plenty of ideas there, but it may be that they have not been in the habit of expressing them, because they have not been accustomed to being asked.

So say, "Hey, Willie, don't just sit there like a wart on a nose. Think!"

"Well, I was just wondering whether we could do . . ."

"Great, Willie, and then we could do . . ."

"Yeah, but what about . . . ?"

"Well, that would be no problem because . . ."

This is what I love to hear. But be careful you don't find yourself looking down your evangelical nose and muttering, "Ridiculous! Nonsense! We tried that years ago. Didn't work." Get the ideas down on paper. Delegate responsibility to Willie and his kin to develop the ideas and *see that they do them.*

To summarize. Learn to recognize and respect the potential that God has stored for the church in the youth He has given to us. Teach them to be responsible by giving them responsibility. Encourage ideas from them, laying those quietly to rest that are no good (and let them see why they are no good), and getting them to follow through on those that are good.

CHAPTER 16

The "Nucleus"

Convoys move at the speed of the slowest ship. So do many youth programs, the reason being, of course, that the prime concern of both is survival for as many as possible. However, the desire for survival can be the biggest factor in not achieving it, as many convoys and churches have discovered.

Defensive thinking can lead to increased vulnerability, and it is necessary to know when to switch from attack to defense and vice versa. In fact, "attack" is often the best means of "defense." The time has come for this switch to take place in many churches. We must begin to think not only of protecting our kids, but also of using them to salvage others. But you will never get all the kids to see this. Many will hang back from any suggestion of reaching others. Some will be totally disinterested. Some will be interested, but inadequate. Some will be as keen as mustard, but their parents will object. Some will be too busy with other activities to devote time to reaching their contemporaries for Christ.

I have met a number of youth leaders who have been discouraged by these obstacles. But I feel they should not be discouraged but rather delighted. You see there is a principle of Christian activity that the church in her mad quest for visible results has tended to overlook. She has been so busy totaling up statistics that she has lost sight of the value of the individual. She has been so intent on building large congregations that she has forgotten how small the Lord's congregation was when He left for heaven. She has majored so completely on the mass that she has overlooked the potential of the nucleus.

Jesus showed us this in His ministry. He put on various spectaculars for the crowds and they came by the thousands. He even put on free bread and fish suppers and on one occasion provided free wine all around. They flocked to Him, but according to Him (and He should know) they came for the excitement and the entertainment value—not for the spiritual blessing.

So He changed His tactics. He withdrew from the crowds, collected His nucleus and began "in-depth" training sessions. Those sessions were a great success. I love the fable about the return of the Lord to heaven. The angels gave Him a fantastic welcome and then gathered around Him, full of questions about His Death, Resurrection and Ascension.

"What's it all about?" they said.

"The redemption of the world," He replied.

"But You've come back here. How will the world know about it?"

"I have trained My men."

"To evangelize the whole world?"

"Yes, indeed, every corner of it."

"How many men did You train for such a mammoth task?"

"A handful."

"A handful? But what if they fail?"

"If they fail, I have no other plans."

"But isn't that a grave risk to take?"

"No, they will not fail."

And they didn't! A tiny handful of the most unlikely characters, enriched with the dynamic of the Living Lord through the presence of the Holy Spirit, did not fail. Witness the church of today! We would not be here if they had failed!

Jesus taught us the value of the individual and the formidable potential of the dedicated nucleus, and we have ignored the principle. The communists didn't ignore it. They took it and used it beautifully to great advantage.

103

Another factor they have learned and capitalized upon is the value of youth. The age range of those joining the Communist Party is between fifteen and twenty-five. In Britain recently the Communist Party held a recruiting drive and reported a good response from fifteen- to seventeen-year olds. In Latin America they get most of their recruits from the high school young people—and when they get them, they don't fool around. They get them in their "cell groups" and start work.

What happened to our thinking? The Lord laid it on the line that you don't get far with a large mass of people. You have to get a dedicated nucleus, and the Communists have used the system so effectively that anyone with only half an eye open can see their remarkable progress in fifty years of existence.

The value of the individual must never be overlooked, and the potential of the dedicated nucleus must be rediscovered. That's why I insist that it does not matter if all your kids don't get excited about an aggressive movement to the unreached. They are helping you select your nucleus! Some youth pastors have told me that if they don't run the right kind of a program to keep the kids amused, the parents get after them, and in some instances that I know of, have had them fired. "What do I do then?" they have asked. "Praise God!" I replied. "Praise God that you got out of the entertainment business which you should never have been in, and that now you are free to get into the business you are supposed to be in—the business of producing disciples who will reach the unreached."

"But suppose I do go for a nucleus of kids and concentrate on them. What happens to the others?" That is a common question that I have been asked. My reply is that you should have someone look after the slower moving ships, while the faster moving ones go into training. It may mean a duplication of work, but that in itself is no argument for not doing it. I have been accused of being cold-hearted and unconcerned for the kids who don't want to go along with what I have been outlining. I simply claim the precedent of the Lord, who when His disciples said it was getting too hot for them, let them go. And not only let them go, but asked some of His wavering remnant if they wanted to leave too. You couldn't accuse Him of not caring. In fact, He cared so much that He knew He couldn't afford to go their speed any longer, for if He did, no one would get anywhere.

Some people have said, "You will lose these kids if you don't look after them." There is a simple answer. If you lose them because you start to show them a virile Christianity that is challenging and exciting, it will be because they have no conception of what it is all about. And if that is the case, then you probably never had them, so you couldn't lose them if you never had them. Of course they can stay and learn what it is all about!

When my wife and I started youth work we had about sixty kids coming to see some movies we rented for them. They came, had fun, fooled around in the dark and generally saw to it that we achieved little or nothing. After a few weeks of that we sat down to take stock and came to the unanimous conclusion that we were not reaching our objective and probably never would. So we decided to get a nucleus that meant business in exchange for the gang that didn't. But how to get the nucleus was the problem, until we thought through our objectives and then it was no problem.

We were supposed to be producing healthy, virile Christians. Therefore, the Bible was to be the basis of our activity. We announced, "Next week there will be a Bible study instead of a movie." Boos and catcalls came from all the corners of the room. Next week six came to the Bible study in marked contrast to the sixty who came for the movies. But it was only a matter of time until all six found Christ and then contacted their friends who contacted their friends. And a lovely thing began to happen. Instead of sixty kids running us ragged on their terms, we began to gather a growing bunch of kids on *our* terms. That is basic.

Now, years later, I could take you to all those original six kids, all married and in Christian service. But on the top of that I could introduce you to many of the sixty as well, for as the months and years went by, they came to know Christ one by one, because we had a group of kids who were for real. And everyone knew it and many wanted to be a part of it.

How do you go about training young people so that they commit themselves to Christ and then to His work of reaching the unreached? *First,* strive for a nucleus. Don't be discouraged if it is small, because that will be an advantage. Jesus started off with John and Andrew and seemed perfectly happy because they were soon on the job. *Second,* let the kids know in no uncertain terms what it is you are aiming for. Be clear in your spiritual objectives and make sure that they are as clear to the kids as to you. I remember once after I had preached to a group of young people on the subject of discipleship and "turning the world upside down," a minister came up to me and said, "What are you trying to do? Frighten them all away, so that I won't see them again?"

"On the contrary," I replied. "I am endeavoring to make sure that you will go on seeing them again and dozens more like them." He looked unconvinced until a group of kids came up to me and said, "Man, that was great. We didn't know that Christianity could be so exciting."

That has been the response that I have often received. Many youngsters are amazed that Christianity is more than a list of rules and sitting in rows. They had no idea it could be exciting and lively and achieve something, and when someone tells them they are thrilled. Far from being frightened off, they are more likely to become addicted. I firmly believe that if you take the strong line of Biblical Christianity to modern church kids, you will set more on fire than you will lose!

Third, get your emphasis right! For instance, don't confuse "separation" and "isolation." When our first group of kids began telling their friends, we were embarrassed, because they wanted us to go and tell their friends too. But their friends were to be found in places that "good Christians don't go." So we had to decide what to do. "Do we go to the kids who wanted us to talk to them in the bar of their 'pub' or do we say that Christians shouldn't go into pubs and therefore they would have to stay unreached?" That was a thorny problem for us at that time, because we were confusing "isolation" and "separation." The Biblical doctrine of "separation" insists that a believer should keep himself separate from sin but also insists that a believer should have a ministry to sinners. The un-Biblical doctrine of "isolation" insists that Christians keep themselves separate from sinners.

Jesus handled it wonderfully. He was always separate from sin, but never far from sinners. When Levi, the tax man, was converted, he put on a banquet for his friends and invited the Lord so that He could witness to them. That seemed like a great idea in the Lord's opinion—so He went, but He was frowned upon by the religious authorities because in their book He should not have been there.

I remember reading about Cassandra, a particularly incisive writer for the *Daily Mirror,* having a high old time lampooning Billy Graham during the Harringay Crusade in London. Eventually he threw down a challenge to Dr. Graham to meet him in a pub for a drink. This was highly publicized, and the "Church" and the "World" waited for the evangelist's response. It was masterly and Biblical. He went—and drank lemonade! Separate from sin and in touch with sinners! I think that Cassandra got quite a shock when the preacher

107

showed up, and there is no doubt he was deeply impressed both by the man he met and the message he heard. There must be a right emphasis in this area with the young people.

It will be necessary to use great discretion as to where you take them because an unwise decision can do a lot of damage, as much damage to the Christian kids, as not going does to the other kids. And please notice that I said, "Where you *take* them" not "where you *send* them!"

Another point that needs to be straightened out is the emphasis on "employment" rather than "enjoyment." As I have visited many churches I have been in a privileged position to see the kind of activities that are arranged by the churches for their kids, and I must say that on countless occasions I have been dismayed. The whole list of activities sounds more like an advertisement for a holiday camp than a training ground for spiritual warriors. I know that young people need their fun, and I agree they should have an all-around approach to life which means that the church has a responsibility to give them social opportunities as well as spiritual training. Nevertheless I feel that many churches have their emphasis totally wrong and spend much more time, effort and money on entertaining the young people than they do on employing them.

Another thing! Why do we always assume that employment and enjoyment are incompatible? If we find a way of employing the kids in such a fashion that they enjoy it, then something real can be achieved. Right from the beginning of our work with young people we made it clear that we believed they had a spirit, soul and body *and in that order*. That meant our approach would be: First, spiritual, because the spirit is of prime importance; Second, social, because the soul is of secondary importance; and Third, physical, because the body comes third in order of importance.

In addition we pointed out to the young people that

there are hundreds of clubs catering to the body and we weren't about to try to compete. We reminded them of the multitudinous facilities made available for social activities, and we couldn't afford to compete. And we explained to them that none of these organizations have anything to offer the spirit, and therefore, it would be criminal for us to ignore our peculiar responsibility while trying to do badly what the other organizations were doing well.

They went along with that thinking, so we encouraged them to think of activities that they would like to do. Then we told them to figure out the specific spiritual objective they would have in doing it. If they could think of one, we did it. If they couldn't, we scrapped it. It is amazing how many activities you can do that are fun and have a specific spiritual objective as well! When you have your kids thinking this way, they will start coming up with ideas, and you will have to sit down with them to evaluate the ideas. Then they may come up with a statement like one girl did and say, "I can do ballet, how can I use that for a spiritual objective?" Then someone will tell you that they are gifted in a certain area, and you will be confronted with the fact that if they are, then God gave them that gift to be used, and you had better use it! This will give you plenty of food for thought.

It will also reveal all kinds of hidden talent. Some of it hidden, because it was hidden to the person who had it! Other talents will be hidden, because the person concerned may feel he couldn't be used. A boy came to me one day and said, "I am a graduate of an art college with a degree in design, but the people in my church were against me going to study art, so I never felt that I could offer my talent to the Lord."

"Why do you think He gave it to you?" I asked him.

"I've been led to question if He did," was the startling reply.

109

We put him to work, and he designed one of our coffee bars for us. It was such a remarkable job that we were approached by a number of commercial coffee houses to see if we would sell ours to them, as it was so far superior to anything they had seen. We told them that we would love to sell it, but unfortunately we didn't think we should as we had borrowed the premises. Needless to say, that young man not only invested his God-given talent and achieved a valuable piece of work with a clear spiritual end but he thoroughly enjoyed himself as well.

Another point that I have found needs to be made clear is the emphasis on "revival" rather than "survival." It is perfectly natural and selfish to be more concerned about your own welfare than that of other people. But it is not right. Any Christian who is wrapped up in himself will be a weak, immature specimen, and it may not be his fault, because he may have been told constantly from the pulpit about the terrible world he lives in and how he must be careful, or it will gobble him up. He has never been encouraged to see the outside world as a mission field and a challenge, but as an ogre and a threat.

Some pastors stand before their people Sunday after Sunday and call them "sheep" and tell them about the wolves waiting for them outside. Jesus told His men they were sheep and that the wolves were waiting and then He said to the sheep, "Go get them." And off they went. Sheep after wolves! I think that is as exciting as it is unusual. Jesus put the emphasis where it belongs. On *revival,* not *survival.*

There is something wholesome about a Christian who believes that he is not only available to people, but also expendable for God. That kind of Christian has no time to become an evangelical hypochondriac, prone to every spiritual disease, beating a continual track to a succession of counselors' offices, worried and defeated by all his real or imagined difficulties.

110

An old Chinese proverb has it, "I grumbled when I had no shoes, until I saw a man who had no feet." Look at the foot-less, and you will have no time to worry about being shoe-less.

I remember a girl who had an awful time when she became a Christian. She was terribly introspective, had all kinds of fears and doubts and was continually in need of someone to prop her up to meet the next calamity that would inevitably appear. In the end as a desperate gamble I decided the only thing I could think of was to put her in charge of a group of younger kids, make her responsible for them and keep an eye on them and her. It worked like a dream. She had no time for her own problems, because she became so busy with theirs. Her worries disappeared, and in their place came a lovely concern for her little flock. She had her emphasis right.

There is such an appalling need and there are such fantastic opportunities today. It is almost criminal that so many churches are pandering to people whose sole problem is selfishness, and it is about time we pointed this out to our kids. Put them on the spot when they come to you next time with some little problem. Tell them about a real problem. Introduce them to someone who is in big trouble. Give them a vision of God cutting loose through them to the other person and get them excited about the possibility of being God's spearhead of blessing instead of God's perennial ailing child.

So there are some of the basic necessities which I consider imperative. Don't try to move an immovable mass. Work from a dedicated nucleus. Don't be mealy-mouthed about your objectives. Tell them how it is— as it is—where it is, till they see it as clearly as you do. Don't be confused in your emphasis. First things, first! Second things if and when you have time—*and good hunting!*

CHAPTER 17

The Triple Stress

Sometimes major objectives are so remote they have no sense of immediacy and therefore engender no real anticipation of achievement. It is necessary to have subsidiary goals. Young people may not be too fired up about a general objective as high sounding as "reaching the unreached of this corner of the vineyard," so it may be necessary to come up with something else that will be part of that objective but more concrete and more readily attainable.

I would suggest three things. First, stress to the nucleus that consistency of life is one of the most important characteristics that will need looking into. Jesus did a great job on the Demoniac of Gadara, got rid of the demons, clothed him, placated him, motivated him and then refused him his request to stay with Him. Instead He told him to go and start an outreach in his home area which he did. There was a great response to his ministry, and it couldn't have been solely due to his exposition of truth because he didn't know very much. People were impressed because he no longer lived in the tombs and snapped chains and frightened the living daylights out of everyone. There was a clear demonstration of a transforming experience that was evident for all to evaluate. People were able to see he was for real. There cannot be too much emphasis on this point.

One young man who had been converted to Christ right out of the dope, sex, commune scene was troubled as he came to see me. He said, "I feel as if I am no longer making the impact on people that I did when I came to Christ a few months ago. This disturbs me greatly." We began to try to discover why it might be. I suggested that there might be some sin in his life that he was unwilling to deal with. He didn't know of anything. I suggested some area of unwillingness that might be a blockage in his spiritual experience, but he couldn't think of anything specific. So I asked him about his hair. He looked startled, and to be quite honest I was even a little startled myself!

His hair was quite the longest I have ever seen on a man. It was longer than waist length and blazing blond. As a concession to the people in the church, he tied it back with a velvet bow on Sundays which made him look like Douglas Fairbanks in one of the midnight movies. "Why do you ask about my hair?" he said.

"Because you have to have a good reason for growing it like that, and I am interested to know what it is."

"I have no idea why I grow it like this. I have never thought of a reason. Do I have to have a reason?" he went on.

"Let me suggest some possible reasons," I replied. *Reason No. 1.* You like it like that. *Reason No. 2.* You want to be noticed so desperately that you have to be so way out, otherwise you would not be noticed. *Reason No. 3.* You have a feeling that you may want to return to your old life someday, and you would want some of your symbolic hair on your head when you arrived. So it is an insurance against backsliding. If Reason No. 1 is the reason, then go ahead, but you'll be awful hot this summer. If it is Reason No. 2, then your real problem is pride and that is the blockage. If it is Reason No. 3, then it is lack of commitment and that is the blockage."

He thought for a minute and said, "I wear it to be noticed and that is pride. I wear it as an insurance against going back and that is lack of commitment. My pride and my lack of commitment are contradicting

113

what I say, and that is why I am ineffective. Thanks!" He got up and left.

Next morning he was in church with his hair cut, but with his straggy beard still there. "Boy!" he said, "what a struggle it was to part with my hair until I saw what a hindrance it was to me and my witness. And then what a joy it was to get rid of it. But I had to keep my beard!"

"Great," I replied, "I'm glad you did what God told you to do. Now look out for the flow of blessing that will come from your life." That night he came minus his beard, looking like a newly plucked chicken. Everyone laughed, and he took an awful ribbing, but deep in his heart he knew he had rid himself of the inconsistencies in his life at that time. Now he is in training for the ministry.

As I'm sure you understand, I am not saying his hair style was sin. But for him the reasons for his long hair were sins, and they had to be resolved. Unfortunately for him there was only one way to resolve them and that was with a pair of scissors! Stress *consistency!*

Secondly, it is imperative that we stress intelligent believing. Many kids believe what they believe simply because they have been told to believe it. They have been too mentally lazy or too spiritually asleep to bother thinking about what they believe. What you believe is important, but so is *why* you believe. The teachings of some churches have almost suggested that to look into their faith intelligently is the same as looking into it liberally. Nonsense! Any faith that cannot be looked into intelligently is hardly worth having and certainly cannot be transmitted.

Therefore, the young people should be encouraged to learn by dialogue as well as monologue. They should be encouraged to think for themselves. They should be made to come up with ideas. They should be given the opportunity of wrestling with awkward problems and thinking through difficult issues. Some leaders find this difficult and therefore won't do it. It is much more challenging to be faced with a group of young people who are alert and alive, thinking and questioning, than it is to have a group of kids sitting like peas in a pod, mute and myopic. But it has to be done!

Of course, some leaders feel that if they cannot answer every question they are letting the kids down. On the contrary, to answer, "I don't know," when you don't, is so refreshing to the kids that they think, *At last there's someone who is honest enough to admit he doesn't know. I'm going to listen to him.*

On occasions I have been asked questions, and I have been tempted to give the "standard answer." Unfortunately, I am not always too convinced of the standard answers myself, so I usually say something like, "Some people say this. Others feel this way. The majority think you ought to feel this way. But to be perfectly frank, I am not impressed with any of these answers. I don't know. What do you think?"

This approach accomplishes a number of things. It shows that you, yourself, are interested in the question to such a degree that you have taken time to examine many answers to it. It also shows that you are honest enough to be open and fair enough to see the other point of view without knocking it. Then it shows that you are not about to be put in the mold because that is where people say you belong and finally it puts the ball back in the kids' court and gives them food for thought. They appreciate all these things.

One day a group of kids spent the afternoon in my home in England. They raised innumerable questions which we kicked around at great length, and over and over again we came up with the answer that the problem under discussion could only be resolved by "balance." Balance came up in the conversation every few minutes, until finally one boy said to me, "What is the difference between 'balance' and 'compromise?'"

I replied, "I think that balance is the bringing into line of two or more conflicting or contradictory aspects of a problem, assuming them to be of equal validity. But compromise is the bringing into line of something invalid with those beliefs which are valid."

"Tremendous!" he replied. "Now tell us what it really is?"

"Okay" I said, catching the spirit of his statement. "If I do it, it's balance, and if you do it, it's compromise."

"Fair enough," he laughed, "that's what I thought!" We had fun and seriousness mixed together—open-mindedness and the pooling of insight. And there are few types of discussions I enjoy more than this.

On the other hand, there are young people in "sound" churches who would be threatened by such an approach. I remember a lovely young American girl giving her testimony to a group of raw youngsters in England. She gave a sweet little talk, but said nothing that they understood because she dealt exclusively with evangelical cliches and spoke in ecclesiastical language that was as meaningful to them as Japanese. However, she was pretty and had a cute accent so they were polite. When she had finished, I thanked her and then said, "You mentioned that you were saved when you were ten."

"Right," she said.

"Some of these young people immediately thought you must have been drowning because that is the only context in which they have heard the word used."

"Oh, no," she laughed. "Jesus came into my heart."

"Good! Would you tell them what you mean by that statement." She flushed, looked at her pretty little shoes, shuffled and whispered, "I can't. I don't know what I mean." She was a typical product of a church that had not concentrated on intelligent believing. That kind of youngster with the best will in the world will never make many inroads into the modern youth situation. Incidentally, the last time I saw the young lady, now a young wife and mother, she thanked me for that embarrassing evening and told me how that experience started her thinking through her faith.

The third factor that needs to be in the forefront of our thinking, as we train people to be effective, is fluent witnessing. I believe that this is dependent to a large degree on the two other factors being understood. We don't need to talk about "fluency of witnessing" if there is blatant inconsistency of life. And needless to say there will be no fluency without an intelligent grasp of the truth.

I feel we should be clear in our thinking as to what witnessing really is. Many people seem to think that it is the repetition of the story of their conversion experience, but I believe it is much more than that. Certainly any adequate witness must include some explanation of the experience of regeneration that the witness has had, but I am convinced that witnessing means the sharing of the reality of the Word of God in a person's life. My emphasis has always been to encourage people to know their Bible and to explain it to people illustrating the validity of what they are saying by their own experience. Unfortunately it is not uncommon to find young and old Christians being encouraged to repeat the same story over and over again but never to give the "meat of the matter" from the Word of God.

"Faith comes by hearing and hearing by the thrilling testimony of some way-out kid." No, not that way, but "by the Word of God." I do not mean to imply that a young person must have a diploma from a Bible school showing that he is qualified to share the Word with people before he may open his mouth, but I do insist that new Christians should immediately be introduced to a deep study of the Bible and then be given every opportunity to share what they have discovered. Some of the best meetings I have attended have been those where new Christians were asked as they entered the meeting to be ready to share with the group the discoveries they had learned from the Bible since last we met together.

I have seen startled looks come over the faces of pastors when I have suggested that we preachers ought to do that regularly because many of them are short on "fresh" Bible themselves. On the other hand, the kids I am telling you about had been trained to expect to be given the opportunity to share their own exciting discoveries and thus they were not only motivated to study, but also they became rapidly proficient in communicating the discoveries.

One final note! Encourage the older people in your group to join in with the young people in this kind of program. They won't fall over themselves to get there, but remember the nucleus! Then when you have the thrill of winning the "outside" young people to the Lord, introduce them to this kind of program too. In this way, you will build up a group of people earnest about the Lord, and the group will contain the children of deacons, the way-out kids, the pastor, some moms and dads, squares and hippies, students and seekers. The Lord will be present and He will bless them all. The group will grow and influence the church. Depth of feeling and commitment will become more important than external matters, and in a very short time I believe you will have the joy of integrating the unreached generation in your church. Then if you will only be patient, you will see some of them head for Bible school and seminary and become pastors and missionaries, doctors and nurses. That is exciting, and God has been good enough to let us see these events actually happen.

CHAPTER 18

All These Kids in Church?

How would you explain it?
The latest fad?
An emotional upheaval?
Communist infiltration?
Spiritual revival?
All those kids in church!
Unashamed,
Unabashed,
Undismayed,
Unbelievable!
Listening,
Learning,
Loving,
Yearning.
Togetherness
Foreverness
Warm smiles,
Quiet eyes,
Serene expression,
Deep impression.
Sharing,
Caring,
Bearing,
Daring,
But where are the old folks?
Some with
Bowed head,
Faces red,
Fled!
Some dismayed,
Afraid,
Prayed and
Stayed.
Knees shaking,
Hearts breaking,
Efforts making,

Chances taking,
To believe,
To receive,
To achieve,
To relieve.
Willing,
Watching,
Waiting,
Worrying,
Saints.
White hair,
Long hair,
No hair,
Tinted hair
Bowed
In prayer.
Weeping together,
Reaping together,
Sowing together,
Growing together.
Lord's work,
Team work.
Worship,
Fellowship,
Relationship,
Stewardship,
Discipleship.
One body,
One Spirit,
One hope,
One Lord,
One faith,
One baptism,
One God,
One Father
Above them all,
Through them all,
And in them all,
AMEN.